DATE			

Modern Peacemakers

Desmond Tutu

Fighting Apartheid

MODERN PEACEMAKERS

Modern Peacemakers

Desmond Tutu

Fighting Apartheid

Samuel Willard Crompton

CHELSEA HOUSE PUBLISHERS

An imprint of Infobase Publishing

Chelsea House
An imprint of Infobase Publishing
132 West 31st Street
New York NY 10001

ISBN-13: 978-0-7910-9221-7

Library of Congress Cataloging-in-Publication Data
Crompton, Samuel Willard.
    Desmond TuTu : fighting apartheid / Samuel Willard Crompton.
       p. cm. — (Modern peacemakers)
    Includes bibliographical references and index.
    ISBN 0-7910-9221-6 (hardcover)
    1. Tutu, Desmond. 2. Church of the Province of South Africa—Bishops—Biography.
3. Anglican Communion—South Africa—Bishops—Biography. 4. Apartheid—South
Africa. 5. South Africa—Race relations. 6. South Africa—Church history. I. Title.
    BX5700.6.Z8T8732 2006
    283.092—dc22
    [B]   2006017556

Chelsea House books are available at special discounts when purchased in bulk quantities for businesses, associations, institutions, or sales promotions. Please call our Special Sales Department in New York at (212) 967-8800 or (800) 322-8755.

You can find Chelsea House on the World Wide Web at
http://www.chelseahouse.com

Series design and composition by Annie O'Donnell
Cover design by Takeshi Takahashi
Cover printed by Yurchak Printing, Landisville, Pa.
Book printed and bound by Yurchak Printing, Landisville, Pa.
Printed in the United States of America

This book is printed on acid-free paper.

All links and Web addresses were checked and verified to be correct at the time of publication. Because of the dynamic nature of the Web, some addresses and links may have changed since publication and may no longer be valid.

TABLE OF CONTENTS

CHAPTER 1

Soweto

In the spring of 1976, Desmond Tutu was gravely concerned about the state of race relations in his homeland, South Africa. He had spent a number of years living and working in different countries—primarily Great Britain—and he was appalled by the indifference of prosperous whites toward poor blacks in South Africa. He was then dean of the Anglican Church in Johannesburg, the largest city in the nation. In May 1976, Tutu wrote an open letter to South African prime minister John Vorster, imploring him to take corrective action before it was too late.

> I am writing to you, sir, because I know you to be a loving and caring father and husband, a doting grandfather who has experienced the joys and anguish of family life, its laughter and gaiety, its sorrows and pains. I am writing to you, sir, as one who is passionately devoted to a stable and happy family life as the indispensable foundation of a sound and healthy society.[1]

Tutu knew a lot about family life. He was happily married and the father of four children. His letter went on:

1

Prime Minister of South Africa John Vorster is pictured above (left) with Rhodesian Prime Minister Ian Smith. In the spring of 1976, around when this photograph was taken, Desmond Tutu wrote to Vorster to voice his concerns about the state of race relations in South Africa. Vorster was unmoved by Tutu's appeals.

I am writing to you, sir, as one who is a member of a race that has known what it has meant in frustrations and hurts, in agony and humiliation, to be a subject people. The history of your own race speaks eloquently of how utterly impossible it is, when once the desire for freedom and self-determination is awakened in a people, for it to be quenched or to be satisfied with anything less than freedom and that self-determination.[2]

By this, Tutu meant that Prime Minister John Vorster was a member of the Afrikaner group, which had previously been subject to the British government. John Vorster's ancestors had fought for their freedom at the start of the twentieth century, and Desmond Tutu hearkened back to this struggle to show the prime minister that blacks and Afrikaners were not very different.

> I write to you, sir, because, like you, I am deeply committed to real reconciliation with justice for all, and to peaceful change to a more just and open South African society.[3]

Reconciliation and justice were key words for Desmond Tutu. Throughout his lifetime, he tried to educate South Africans to strive for reconciliation instead of revenge, and for justice rather than retribution.

He continued:

> I am writing to you, sir, because I have a growing nightmarish fear that unless something drastic is done very soon then bloodshed and violence are going to happen in South Africa almost inevitably. A people can take only so much and no more.[4]

Though he did not mention it by name, Tutu referred to the policy of *apartheid*, or "apart-ness," which defined a strict separation between the racial groups in South Africa. Though he was a black South African, Tutu spoke for the three underprivileged minorities in South Africa: the blacks, the coloreds (the South African term for people of mixed racial descent), and the Indians. All three groups suffered under apartheid, but blacks had it the worst in that they could not move or travel about without carrying a passbook. If a black person was found outside of a designated black area without this permit, he or she could be arrested. The pass laws had come about in the 1930s, and Desmond Tutu and his friends saw them as one of the worst signs of racial injustice in their homeland.

We blacks are exceedingly patient and peace-loving. We are aware that politics is the art of the possible. We cannot expect you to move so far in advance of your voters that you alienate their support. We are ready to accept some meaningful signs which would demonstrate that you and your government and all whites really mean business when you say you want peaceful change.[5]

Desmond Tutu's critics would claim that his black countrymen were not peace-loving. There had been occasional outbursts of violence over the past decade, and the white minority group in South Africa had heavily armed itself, both at the national and the household level, to resist being overthrown. Tutu's critics could also claim that he was running away from the struggle because he was about to leave his beloved South Africa to live in the neighboring country of Lesotho.

This flows from a deep love and anguish for my country. I shall soon become bishop of Lesotho, when I must reside in my new diocese. But I am quite clear in my own mind, and my wife supports me in this resolve, that we should retain our South African citizenship no matter how long we have to remain in Lesotho.[6]

Citizenship was a key element of the struggle between whites and blacks. Under a plan called the grand apartheid movement, which was first outlined in a government commission in the 1950s, blacks were to be stripped of their South African citizenship and allowed to reside only in black tribal "homelands." These homelands comprised about 13 percent of the land of South Africa. Generations of black Africans had grown up in the cities and suburbs of South Africa and had never even seen their "homeland."

Please may God inspire you to hear us before it is too late, and may he bless you and your government now and always.[7]

The June 1976 riots and subsequent massacre in Soweto inspired activism across South Africa. In the photograph above, marchers in Cape Town are shown protesting against police treatment of black South Africans on September 4, 1976.

Prime Minister John Vorster did not listen to Desmond Tutu's appeal. In a curt reply, he suggested that Tutu's letter was politically motivated. Just five weeks after the letter was sent, some of the terrible things that Desmond Tutu had warned of came to pass.

THE SOWETO RIOTS

The name "Soweto" is an acronym for the southwestern townships around Johannesburg. The southwestern townships included a large group of blacks-only residential areas, from which black workers commuted into the city of Johannesburg to work. Many of the townships previously had individual names, but the number of people coming to live in them had grown to such an extent that it was easier to lump them together with the single name Soweto.

When Americans remember the year 1976, they usually think of it as their bicentennial year. This was the year when the United States celebrated its 200th anniversary. For South Africans, however, 1976 will always be remembered as the year of the Soweto riots.

About 750,000 blacks resided in greater Soweto. They lived in squalid conditions compared to their white counterparts, who lived in suburbs around Johannesburg. Even so, there was a vitality about life in Soweto that people loved and admired. In the spring of 1976, though, Soweto was a very troubled place, and everything was about to get a lot worse.

That spring, the Afrikaner government decreed that black students in Soweto would be instructed in Afrikaans as well as in English. Afrikaans, the Afrikaner language, was seen by blacks as the language of the oppressor, and most did not wish to learn it. Riots began on June 16, 1976, the anniversary of a black resistance movement that had begun in 1952. The young protestors had been born in the years shortly after 1952. They saw the thwarted dreams of that year as something they needed to address.

Thousands of people ran into the streets. Most were black, and nearly all were teenagers or children. They threw rocks and screamed. They danced, making defiant gestures. These rioting young students might have been relatively safe if the local police alone had intervened. Instead, however, the South African government decided that the student movement must be crushed, and they sent the military into Soweto.

First the soldiers fired tear gas. Then they began using live ammunition. Dozens, perhaps hundreds, of children were killed or wounded in a short time. One of the first to fall was 13-year-old Hector Peterson. Another black teenager carried Peterson in his arms, while Peterson's sister ran alongside weeping. A photograph of this scene was picked up by the Associated Press news agency and the picture spread to the rest of the world. For the first time, people in America, Europe, and other parts of the world could put a face on the evils of apartheid.

Commentary appeared in American newspapers the next day. There was much to discuss about Africa: There was famine in Rhodesia (now known as Zimbabwe), a civil war in Ethiopia, and now a black student revolt in Soweto. At another time, Americans might have forgotten about Soweto because there were so many other events commanding world attention. That photograph of Hector Peterson being carried in his friend's arms, and the vivid memories of Americans' own civil rights struggle a decade earlier, however, combined to make Americans much more aware of South Africa. Although it would take some time, Americans began to respond. As a result, American corporations slowly began to reduce their investments in South Africa, which weakened the economic power of the oppressors.

Desmond Tutu was in Johannesburg when the Soweto riots exploded. He rushed to Soweto and was appalled by what he saw. He pleaded with police, the military, and the white Afrikaner government to pull back from Soweto, but he was not yet the famous religious leader who could influence these events. At that moment, he was dean of the Diocese of Johannesburg, and he was about to leave the country to become bishop of Lesotho. His plans to leave weakened his position, and he did not have much of an effect on the situation.

Tutu left for Lesotho a few weeks later. The mountain kingdom is completely encircled by the nation of South Africa, and Tutu would be able to observe events from very close by. He left his homeland at a time of great crisis and doubtless felt grave concern over this, but he knew in his heart that he would return.

CHAPTER 2

Humble Beginnings

Desmond Tutu was born in Klerksdorp (which was then in Transvaal), South Africa, on October 7, 1931. His parents were Zachariah and Aletha Tutu. Tutu was born into a rather harsh world. Two generations before, Klerksdorp had been a prosperous gold mining town, but it was now mired in depression. The entire nation was about to enter the worldwide Great Depression of the 1930s. The economic situation was difficult for all, but it fell hardest on the minority peoples of South Africa.

Desmond Tutu grew up in a multiethnic household. His father was a Xhosa tribesman from the Eastern Cape Province, and his mother was from a different tribe, which spoke Tswana. Because their Sotho-speaking grandmother lived with them, no less than three languages were spoken in the Tutu household. Consequently, Desmond Tutu grew up hearing and speaking a number of languages, and this gave him the ability to learn new languages easily throughout his life. He would eventually learn and speak about eight languages in all.

By all accounts, Desmond Tutu was a happy little boy. He was not physically robust. In fact his grandmother gave him the middle name of *Mpilo* ("life") to encourage the young boy. Small and slight for his age, Desmond was a joyful child all the same. He ran, danced, and sang, just like his peers. South Africans, black and white, are a noticeably athletic and vibrant people. White South Africans delight in organized sports like rugby, whereas black South Africans are adept at dance, song, and movement. Desmond was no exception to the rule; he was a fun-loving youngster.

Desmond had two sisters: one older and one younger. When his older sister enrolled at a prestigious Anglican high school, the entire Tutu family converted from the Methodist faith to the Anglican one. The family did not see much conflict in this move; the Methodist and Anglican faiths had been the ones most active in converting black tribespeople of South Africa, and many moved readily from one Christian faith to the other. Nonetheless, this would be a decision that would impact the rest of Tutu's life, for when he entered the church, it would be Anglican.

If there was a shadow over his early years, it was social and familial rather than economic. The Tutu family was poor, but so were all their neighbors, and no one saw any shame in it. Zachariah Tutu was a local schoolteacher, an important position in the community. Desmond Tutu grew up with some security, in that he knew his father was an important man in the local area. His father got drunk often, however, and he sometimes beat his wife. This caused young Desmond so much pain that he did not speak of it until later in life and usually could not do so without tears. Having witnessed violence in his home, Tutu would always reject violence in his own life, and he would become an outspoken advocate for the underdog and the downtrodden.

Demond's mother, Aletha, was a washerwoman, working for white families in the nearby suburbs. Perhaps it pained the young boy to see his mother doing this menial work, but her lot was similar to that of most black women. Desmond came to identify more with his mother than with his father. Although he yearned to be a man of importance, and a man of letters like his father, Desmond Tutu's greater concern would always be the struggle for peace and justice.

When the family moved to the town of Roodepoort, Aletha Tutu got a new job as a cook at the Ezenzeleni School for the Blind. A British couple founded and ran the school, the first such place for black South Africans. Desmond often went there with his mother and was impressed by the kindness of the people there. Years later, he wrote to the British couple that they had no idea how much good will they had sown in the early years of his childhood.

From the beginning, Desmond was an excellent student. His schoolteacher father made sure there were plenty of books and magazines in their home, and one of Desmond Tutu's early memories of racial pride was of reading about American baseball player Jackie Robinson in the magazine *Ebony*. Like most South Africans, Desmond knew very little about baseball because cricket was the national sport of South Africa. But he was thrilled to learn about this American black man who had done so well in desegregating the formerly all-white baseball leagues.

The Tutu family moved several times during his youth. His father's career advanced to school administration, and he took better jobs and moved the family closer to Johannesburg. These moves were probably beneficial for young Desmond because he was able to see more townships and different social conditions. He also became more aware of racial prejudice, however, and one of his most painful experiences was watching several white South African boys taunting his middle-aged father. They called the schoolteacher "boy," and showed their disrespect in every way they could. There was nothing Zachariah Tutu could do in this situation; all black South Africans had to put up with such behavior.

One could certainly ask why the racial divide had become so deep. As Desmond Tutu noted in his 1976 letter to Prime

Father Trevor Huddleston is shown in this photograph from 1960. Huddleston was a British priest who became one of the first leaders of the resistance against South African apartheid. Huddleston's dignified activism inspired young Desmond Tutu to pursue justice in his homeland.

Minister John Vorster, the Dutch Afrikaners had themselves been an oppressed people. They had first come to South Africa in 1652 and had run much of the country for some time, but the British came and displaced them in 1820. After a long period of shaky peace, the two peoples had fought the Anglo-Boer War of 1899–1902. The British won, which left a lasting bitterness among the Dutch Afrikaners. Why would the Afrikaners now turn around and oppress the South African blacks? Perhaps those who have been steadily oppressed look for another group whom they can oppress. Rare has it been that an oppressed people would then turn around and show kindness and magnanimity to others. Throughout his life, Desmond Tutu would strive for such an uplifted and enlightened attitude; this is one of the characteristics that makes him so remarkable.

One of the first positive images Desmond Tutu had of white people came from a British priest named Trevor Huddleston. A member of the Community of the Resurrection, founded at Oxford University in 1892, Huddleston came to South Africa in 1943, and it was probably one year later that the 12-year-old Desmond Tutu saw this British priest remove his hat out of respect to Desmond's mother. This was the first time young Desmond had ever seen a white man show deference or respect toward a black woman, and he remembered it for the rest of his life.

Trevor Huddleston described the black township of Sophiatown in his remarkable book *Naught for Your Comfort*:

> They say that Sophiatown is a slum. Strictly in terms of the slums act they are absolutely correct, for the density of the population is about twice what it should be—70,000 instead of 30,000. But the word slum to describe Sophiatown is grossly misleading and especially to people who know the slums of Europe or the United States. It conjures up immediately a picture of tenement buildings, old and damp, with crumbling stone and dark cellars.[8]

That was not the Sophiatown Father Huddleston knew. Like many inhabitants of the black townships, he knew a lively, vibrant place, where homes housing three generations were the norm rather than the exception.

> You see, moving up and down the hilly streets, people and groups: people with colorful clothes; people who, when you come up to them, are children playing, dancing, and standing around the braziers. And above it all you see the Church of Christ the King, its tower visible north, south, east, and west riding like a great ship at anchor.[9]

Father Huddleston loved Sophiatown, especially its children:

> The Sophiatown child is the friendliest creature on earth and the most trusting. God knows why it should be so, but it is. You'll be walking across the playground and suddenly feel a tug on your sleeve or a pressure against your knee; and then there will be a sticky hand in yours. "Hallo, Farther, hallo, Seester, how are you? Hallo, hallo, hallo. . ." you will come back from Johannesburg, as I have done a thousand times, fed up and sick with weariness from that soulless city, and immediately you are caught in a rush and scurry of feet, in faces pressed against the car window, in arms stretching up to reach yours whether you like it or not. You are *home*.[10]

Desmond Tutu was one of these children.

Later in life, Tutu often described himself as a street urchin in his childhood. He scampered about, played card tricks, rode the streetcars and railroads, and had numerous friends. There was nothing to distinguish him from his peers. His father was indeed a prestigious member of the community, but Desmond Tutu lived an entirely normal childhood. He was one of those children whom Father Huddleston heard in the rush and scurry of feet, one of those whose arms pressed against the car window—until he fell ill with tuberculosis.

Tuberculosis, a bacterial disease also called consumption, was one of the great killers of the time. People often spent years

Influences on the Peacemaker

British priest Trevor Huddleston was, beyond doubt, the single most important influence in launching Tutu along the path toward the Nobel Peace Prize. There are some who contend that Huddleston should himself have won such an award, perhaps back in the 1950s when his was one of the few voices raised against apartheid.

Born in London in 1913, Huddleston came from a distinguished British family. His father was an important British military leader in India, and Trevor did not see his father until he was seven years old. The strongest influence on his own young life was that of his very religious mother, who steered him to active participation in the Anglican Church.

During the 1930s, Huddleston was at Oxford, where, like many of his peers, he became interested in the Roman Catholic roots of the Church of England. He joined the Community of the Resurrection, becoming a priest in 1936. But the most formative experience of his life began in 1943 when a superior decided he should go to South Africa to minister to the needs of the Anglican mission community around Johannesburg.

Nothing could have prepared Huddleston for the contrasts he experienced in making his weekly rounds. The British and Dutch communities around Johannesburg were prosperous, and, in a word, dull, while the black African townships teemed with life.

Huddleston threw himself into this work with a tremendous will and vitality. Nelson Mandela, who lived in Johannesburg at the time, remembered that Father Huddleston was one of the few persons— black or white—who boldly walked around the black townships at night, because his fearless reputation had preceded him.

In the early 1950s, Father Huddleston led the fight to keep Sophiatown what it was, a black township outside Soweto. He

not knowing they had contracted the disease, but once it came on, they would slowly cough their lungs out and die a painful death. Desmond was one of the lucky ones in that doctors located his disease early and he had a plan of treatment. He had to leave home

wrote *Naught for Your Comfort* to show the rest of the world what was happening to South African blacks because of apartheid. But his superiors decided he was too exposed—that the South African government might arrest and detain him—so he was recalled to Britain.

After a lightning-fast tour of the United States, in which he introduced his many audiences to the evils of apartheid, Father Huddleston worked both in Britain and in central African nations. He returned home by the 1980s and was instrumental in creating the "Free by 70" movement, intended to spring Nelson Mandela from jail.

The liberation of Mandela in 1990 and the start of peace talks between the forces of apartheid and those of black freedom opened the way for Huddleston to return to South Africa. He went back in June 1993, having been away for 36 years. This visit marked a major completion for him, but his last years were not easy ones.

In 1994 Huddleston went to South Africa to retire, but the experiment proved an abject failure. Suffering from diabetes and complications from that disease, Father Huddleston lived in considerable pain. He had always had a quick temper, but in the past he had been quick to apologize and forgive; this was no longer the case. Huddleston returned to England, where he died in 1998. His funeral service was notable for the many dignitaries who attended, but also for the magnificent trumpet solo, performed by a young South African to whom Huddleston had given a trumpet back in 1955.

The South African Parliament unanimously voted to create a memorial in honor of Huddleston, who, it declared, should always be known as "Father Huddleston" for his role in the antiapartheid movement.

and spend a great deal of time in a hospital run by the brothers of the Community of the Resurrection. Treatment for tuberculosis was very demanding in those days, and there were plenty of times during his treatment that Desmond was in despair, but he found consolation in his growing religious beliefs.

Until then, Desmond had gone to church like other boys, but he had not taken it very seriously. Now faced with very serious illness, he became a truly religious person. At one point, faced with his possible death, he simply said to himself: "If I die—then, Okay."[11] Decisions like this can change a person's entire life. Shakespeare wrote long ago, "Be earnest for death, for then either life or death shall be the sweeter." A person who has faced the likelihood of death may be less frightened by the challenges of life.

Father Huddleston also played a big role in Desmond Tutu's recovery. He came to visit the boy at least once a week, usually bringing lots of books and newspapers with him. They shared a great interest in reading and stories, and Father Huddleston lifted the spirits of the young boy. Desmond had already been impressed by hearing Huddleston speak in public a few years earlier. Now he found himself drawn to this charismatic man and to the faith he represented. Father Huddleston understood the black South Africans of the 1940s better than almost any other white person of his time.

Twenty long months of convalescence finally ended when Desmond was 16. Released from the hospital, he went home to resume a normal life. He would always retain some vestiges of his illness. Throughout life, the treatments caused the partial paralysis of his right hand, and he could often be seen pressing the two hands together to stimulate the injured one. Tutu had come close to death, but it made him love life more.

HIGHER EDUCATION

Desmond Tutu had always been a good student, but the 20 months he spent in the hospital made him even more committed to education. He excelled in high school, and the tests he took in senior year indicated that academically, he was in the top half of one percent of all black South Africans of the time. Of course, it must be remembered that few black South Africans attended high school during these years, so the ranking may not be entirely reflective of the population.

Desmond's experience with tuberculosis inspired him to become a physician. South Africa as a whole had a shortage of doctors, but the black community specifically had very few indeed. Desmond searched for scholarship money or some other type of assistance, but there was none. Therefore, at the age of 19, he decided to follow in his father's footsteps and become a schoolteacher. He went to the Bantu Normal School in Pretoria. This was the only college in South Africa that trained black teachers. Tutu and a small number of other students wanted to learn so they could teach other black South Africans. Most of the teachers at the school were white and Afrikaner, and they had a rather condescending attitude toward their black students. As a rule, white South Africans did not think that black South Africans could learn much, and they often watered down their lessons. They also thought that black students should live in physical environments exactly like those of their tribal ancestors. Therefore, the students at Bantu Normal School lived in huts rather than in typical dormitories.

The educational facilities were inadequate, but the spirit among many of the students was high, and Desmond Tutu was one of those. He did not believe in a diluted education at all; he wanted to pursue the finest traditions of academic excellence. He excelled in all his studies except mathematics, which would remain a difficult subject throughout his life.

Perhaps it was fortunate that Desmond Tutu entered college in 1950, and that he was not living in the wider South African society at the time, for 1948, the year in which apartheid began, marked a severe dividing line between the racial groups of the nation. In 1948, the National Party of the Afrikaner people won the overall elections and assumed power of the government for the first time. The National Party had won the election on a platform of the Black Peril. Almost as soon as they had won, the party's leaders announced their program to completely separate the racial groups in South Africa. One of their key expressions was, "the *Kaffir* in his place" (*Kaffir* is a Muslim word meaning "infidel"; the expression was, and is, a racial slur used to demean blacks in Africa).

Two years after the National Party's victory, marriage between the races was prohibited. Within three years, even dating between different racial groups was against the law. Desmond was far enough away not to have to witness all the new aspects of segregation. During this time, Desmond Tutu was working on his studies and preparing for his future life as a teacher.

Desmond played no part in the resistance movement that began in the early 1950s. Leaders of the African National Congress (ANC), founded in 1912, called for boycotts of the white-run industries and transportation systems. The ANC played a similar role to that of the National Association for the Advancement of Colored People (NAACP), founded in the United States in 1910. Young leaders like Nelson Mandela and Walter Sisulu emerged as leaders of the black resistance to apartheid. Desmond Tutu did not know these men at the time, but he would later collaborate with them in the still-larger resistance of the 1970s and 1980s.

The biggest resistance of all came in 1952. White South Africans celebrated the 300th anniversary of the arrival of the Dutch Afrikaners on April 6, 1952. Major celebrations were held in Cape Town, where the first immigrants had arrived. Black leaders such as Nelson Mandela organized a counter-tricentennial to show the terrible effects of 300 years of white rule on the tribal peoples of South Africa. The black resistance led to major strikes, boycotts, and protests on June 16, 1952, later known as Freedom Day, throughout the land. Mandela and many others were arrested. Some, including Mandela, were banned from making any further public speeches.

Nelson and Winnie Mandela are shown above in this photograph from their 1957 wedding. Nelson Mandela was active early on in the black resistance to apartheid in South Africa. Though Tutu did not know Mandela when he organized the 1952 counter-tricentennial, the two men would become friends and allies later in the struggle.

People have often asked Desmond Tutu why he was not more active in these early protest movements. He often expressed a certain frustration with himself, saying that he wonders about that himself. Perhaps it was that he was so involved in his studies; perhaps he and other students at the Bantu Normal School felt they had to "climb" socially to become enough like their white professors to be accepted. Whatever the reason for his lack of engagement in the 1950s, though, Desmond Tutu more than made up for it in the decades to come.

About the time he completed his education, Desmond found the great love of his life. Leah Shenxane had known Desmond in high school. He had not been interested in her at the time, and she remembered him as the rather stuck-up son of a schoolteacher. The two met again at the Bantu Normal School, though, and their acquaintance turned to friendship, and friendship ripened into love. They married in the summer of 1955, just as Tutu was about to start his teaching career.

The couple was so poor that they made their first home in the living room and dining room of Tutu's parents' home. As with many young couples, poverty did not distress them. Their first child was born in 1956 and they called him Trevor, after Father Huddleston. The future seemed bright.

CHAPTER 3

Teacher
and Priest

Marriage agreed with Desmond Tutu. He and his wife, Leah, shared many thoughts, feelings, and aspirations. Both came from the more prosperous group of blacks of their time, and both were ambitious for the future. It is safe to say that Leah was a steadying influence on Desmond from the very beginning and that, without her guiding hand, he might never have become such an inspiration to other people.

At about the time he married, Tutu also began his teaching career. He taught a variety of subjects at Munsieville High School in Krugersdorp. To say that he was an inspiring teacher is an understatement. Tutu had a great love of learning, but for him it was a learning infused with the drama and enthusiasm of childhood. He remained, in many ways, the street urchin, the type of person Father Huddleston had written about in *Naught for Your Comfort*. Tutu loved to show and explain things to his students, but he wanted them to enter into the spirit of what they learned. If they studied Shakespeare, he led them into the pathos of Shakespearean drama.

Tutu's life seemed more complete than ever before. He had come a long way in a short time, and his happiness might have been complete were it not for new actions by the white South African government.

SEPARATE AND UNEQUAL

Americans recall 1954 as the year of the Supreme Court decision *Brown v. Board of Education*. In that landmark ruling, the Court ruled that the doctrine of "separate but equal" was not acceptable with regard to educational facilities for children. From that moment on, there was an ever-increasing movement to desegregate American schools.

Sadly, South Africans do not remember that year as a time of liberation or improvement. Rather, they remember that the Bantu Education Act was passed in 1953 and implemented in 1955. The author of the act, Dr. Hendrik Verwoerd, explained his thinking:

> My department's policy is that Bantu education should stand with both its feet in the reserves [tribal homelands]. What is the use of teaching the Bantu child mathematics when it cannot use it in practice? . . . It is of no avail to him to receive a training which has as its aim absorption in the European community. Until now he has been subject to a school system which drew him away from his own community and misled him by showing him the green pastures of European society in which he is not allowed to graze.[12]

Dr. Verwoerd might have been speaking to Desmond Tutu in person. Tutu was one of the few blacks who had been able to take advantage of the educational system, and now he was trying to open that door to others. The state said no, however: Blacks must be educated for their future as common laborers.

Even worse, the South African government demanded that mission schools—those founded by priests and missionaries like Father Huddleston—revise their syllabuses and teaching methods. No longer could blacks expect to receive a European-style education. If the schools failed to comply, the state would withdraw any financial support for those institutions.

Tutu watched all this with growing anger and despair. Until about 1955, he was a cautious believer in the South African state, thinking things would get better with time. These new moves, so harsh and sudden, showed him that the future was bleak.

Adding injury to insult, the government also announced it would level Sophiatown. This was one of the biggest black townships, and, as Father Huddleston described, an area rich in culture, history, and hope. The white government called Sophiatown a black spot on the map, surrounded by white communities, and said it must be leveled and replaced with a white suburb. Once again, Father Huddleston led the protests:

> Sophiatown *was* a slum. Those of us who have lived there would never wish to deny that. We have seen with our own eyes the heroism of so many of our own Christian people in the battle to fight and to overcome their environment. It would be treason to deny that Sophiatown was a slum. But slum conditions can be removed without the expropriation of a whole area. Indeed the greatest experts in town planning would agree that only in the last resort should you uproot people from the place they know as home. . . . Sophiatown, then, could have been replanned and rebuilt on the same site: a model African suburb.[13]

This did not happen, however. Despite protests and increasing notice from the world community of nations, the South African government leveled Sophiatown and replaced it with a suburb called *Triomf* ("Triumph").

In 1956, Father Huddleston left South Africa. His superiors were afraid he would be harmed if he remained. Desmond Tutu had lost his great mentor and inspiration, but he was older now, and ready to take on a leadership role. In 1956, Tutu decided to leave teaching. He could not agree with the new syllabus mandated for his students; it aimed too low and did not encourage the development of their higher faculties. Tutu did not wish to abandon his students, however. He decided to remain another three years so he could see all those students currently in his charge through to graduation. After that, he would change his career and life. He would become a priest.

The decision was not a huge surprise. Tutu's maternal grandfather had been a minister in a black Protestant church, and the family had been Christian from the outset. The major resistance came from Tutu's father, who was very proud his son had followed him into teaching and did not want to see him leave. Tutu and his wife Leah were determined to maintain their course, however, even though it would entail hardships and sacrifice.

St. Peter's College, in Johannesburg, was about the only place Tutu could go for theological training. Founded by the Community of the Resurrection, St. Peter's had many black students before Tutu, but none who would go on to achieve such fame afterward. He excelled in his studies from the very start. His teaching experience made him a better learner than before, and his grades put him at the head of his class. There was also much time for meditation and prayer, both of which were becoming central in Desmond Tutu's life. He had always believed in God, but in the past, his belief had been distant and vague. His experience with tuberculosis had forced him to draw on spiritual strength within.

There was sorrow in Tutu's life at that time, as well. During the years he studied at St. Peter's, Tutu could not be close to his family. The rules of the college and the family's finances both conspired to keep Tutu and Leah apart. She continued her own education, training to become a nurse, while Tutu's mother, Aletha, took care of their children, son Trevor and daughters Theresa and Naomi.

Tutu passed his exams and received his license in theology in 1960. He was ordained as a deacon in that same year. But his personal success and the joy of reuniting with his family were tainted by what happened in South Africa that spring.

South African Churches

South Africa offers a multiplicity of religions and churches, but the Anglican faith has always drawn the largest percentage of the population.

From 1652, when the Dutch first arrived, the Dutch Reformed Church, a Protestant denomination, was powerful in the western part of the country, the Cape of Good Hope region. The British came over a century later, bringing with them the Anglican faith (the Church of England) and the Methodist faith.

Both groups were instrumental in creating new churches and missions, but the Methodists outstripped the Anglicans in attracting the black community. Desmond Tutu, indeed the whole Tutu family, were Methodists, until they made a simultaneous conversion to Anglicanism. Nelson Mandela, the great fighter against apartheid, was raised a Methodist, and many of the missions in the black countryside were Methodist. In the cities, though, the Anglican faith dominated. There were also Roman Catholics and Jews in South Africa, but neither group was as numerous as the Protestant denominations.

By the time Desmond Tutu decided to become an Anglican priest, the Anglican Church was the most vibrant and successful religious organization in the South African townships. The Dutch Reformed Church had many adherents within the Afrikaner population, but that church was seen as too closely allied with the white government to win many other converts.

Desmond Tutu is pictured here in 1986 with the head of the South African Council of Churches, Beyers Naude (left), and Methodist leader Reverend Peter Story (center). Tutu, an Anglican priest, greatly valued cooperation with other denominations in South Africa.

GROWING PROTEST

Protests against apartheid gained strength in the 1950s. Father Huddleston protested against the destruction of Sophiatown. Leaders such as Nelson Mandela and Albert Luthuli protested the entire system of apartheid. As the protests gained strength, there was a split in the black freedom movement. Previously, there had been one major group: the African National Congress. Now there was a second, rival, group, the Pan-Africanist Congress (PAC).

The latter group moved first, in March 1960. There were freedom movements throughout Africa at the time, and many were succeeding. The first all-black government had recently been elected in the Congo. Taking heart from this and other developments, the PAC led a major resistance protest in the black township of Sharpeville. As the crowd reached about 10,000 strong, the white police responded with alarm. Many were armed with rubber bullets and tear gas, but others had live bullets. By the end of the day, 68 people had been killed and 180 wounded. This was the single worst day of racial conflict South Africa had ever experienced.

Even then, Tutu was not part of the freedom movement. He watched from afar and admired many of the people involved, but his calling seemed so different from theirs. First he had been a teacher, a man who imparted knowledge. Now he was on his way to becoming a priest, one who imparted the word of God. How could he be involved in such violent demonstrations?

After being ordained a priest (the next step after deacon) in 1961, Tutu began preaching in Thokoza, southeast of Johannesburg. The Tutu family was completely reunited now, and Tutu had found his place in life as well as his voice. Just as he had thrived in teaching, he now took to the pulpit and the charge of providing pastoral care.

Tutu might well have stayed in South Africa for the rest of his life. The chances are he would have risen in the Anglican community, but not to a great height, because he lacked the credentials one earned by studying and preaching overseas. Much to his surprise, his chance came in 1962, when Tutu moved with his entire family to London.

Americans think of Washington, D.C., or New York City as being centers of the world, but for English-speaking South Africans—black or white—London was the nerve center. Even if British rule of South Africa had been less than enlightened, there were aspects of British culture, language, and law that most South Africans admired. There was equality before the law within the country, and the assumption that a person is innocent until proven guilty.

Wounded rioters lie in the streets of Sharpeville, South Africa, following an antiapartheid demonstration organized by the Pan-Africanist Congress, which called upon South Africans to leave their passes at home. During the conflict, police killed 68 people and wounded 180 more.

The Tutus were delighted with London and most of the people they met. In South Africa, no matter how what their activities were, the Tutus felt they always lived under a cloud. The growth and strengthening of apartheid had made things much worse during Tutu's lifetime. The change was truly refreshing. He recalled with delight an episode in a British bank: He was in line to be served when a white man went past him and tried to cut in front of him: "As a well-behaved Bantu, I was ready to let this happen when the lady bank clerk told him firmly but politely that I was next. You could have knocked me down with a feather."[14] It took some time for the conditioning of apartheid to wear off. The Tutus were thrilled with the change in their lives, but sometimes they wondered if it could really be true—the changes in their lifestyle were so radical.

Tutu was greatly impressed by Speakers' Corner in Hyde Park. In one of the great parks of central London, a place is set aside for anyone and everyone to get up and speak, on any subject they please. Nothing they say, no matter how radical or strange, can be used to stop them. This may seem a small thing to British or Americans, accustomed to freedom of speech, but for the Tutus it was a revelation. There was no such place in South Africa.

Tutu studied theology at King's College, part of the University of London. Academically, he was in his element. He studied the Old and New Testaments, listened to speeches by renowned theologians, and was never made to feel he was "second class" in any regard. Tutu received his master's in theology in 1963; the degree was handed to him by Elizabeth, the Queen Mother of England, in her role as chancellor of the University. Many people thought he would return home at this point, but he wrote to his mentor that he would like to stay on for a doctorate:

> Please, I hope it does not sound big-headed or, worse, downright silly. But if I go back home as highly qualified as you can make me, the more ridiculous our Government will appear to be to earnest and intelligent people. Away from home we do unfortunately bear the burden of representing our people, who are judged by our achievements or lack of them. I hope this does not sound like something out of Hyde Park Corner.[15]

Tutu did not mention that concern for his family was part of his reason. He and Leah were very happy in Britain, and their children were doing extremely well at school. Being away from the destructive system of apartheid was a boon to all of them. The Tutus stayed in Britain for another three years.

During this time, Tutu was a parish priest, first at Golders Green and then at Bletchingley. The two parishes were very different in that one consisted of working-class parishioners, and the other brought in members of the upper middle class. Tutu did well in both positions. He was a natural as a parish priest. He had an endearing way of learning the names of all his congregants; he often said that, like a good shepherd, he needed to know them one by one, name by name.

For the first time, the Tutus had a house of their own and became accustomed to a middle-class lifestyle. The Tutu children entered private schools and did very well in their studies. Tutu thrived in his new situation. Leah did, as well, and their four children flourished in Britain (Mpho, their third daughter, completed the family). All good things come to an end, however, and in 1966, Tutu went back to South Africa to take up his position as a priest in the Anglican Church. Along the way, he spent three months in Jerusalem, where he refined his master's thesis on the Muslim faith. Tutu truly was an international thinker; he believed Christians needed to know more about Muslims, and he put this belief to the test during his short time in Jerusalem. Tutu was shocked to witness the degree to which Arabs and Jews detested one another. Like many other foreigners, he had originally thought of the creation of the Israeli state as a wonderful thing, but as time passed, he became an outspoken advocate for the Palestinian cause, saying that the Palestinians needed a home of their own. This made him unpopular in some circles.

Returning to South Africa in 1967, Tutu went to work at a college located at Alice, in a tribal homeland in the eastern part of South Africa. He had two worlds: one academic and one religious. There were very few periods in Tutu's life when he did not have two roles at one time.

Tutu had been sheltered during his years in Britain. Now, back in his homeland, he was dismayed by the growth of racism and the increased strength of apartheid throughout the land. When he had left his home in 1962, apartheid was about 12 years old. There had been hopes at that time that the 1960 massacre at Sharpeville and other offenses would persuade the white government to change its mind, but the opposite had occurred. The white South African government had, if anything, become even more resolute in its determination to separate black from white, Indian from colored.

The University College of Fort Hare, close to Alice, had long been one of the few institutions in the country that admitted

South Africa in Tutu's Absence

The four years that Tutu spent in London (1962–1966) were crucial ones in the history of South Africa. When he left, the black resistance forces were gaining strength; but when he returned, they had been almost completely crushed.

Nelson Mandela and other leaders of the African National Congress (ANC) decided on a more militant approach. Mandela formed a military section of the ANC called *Umkhonto we Sizwe,* meaning "Spear of the Nation." Going overseas, Mandela underwent training in methods of sabotage and prepared to become a revolutionary leader, like Fidel Castro or Che Guevara of Cuba. On his return to South Africa, Mandela was quickly captured. He and about nine other defendants were put on trial for sabotage; the trial was held in Pretoria.

Mandela made a riveting speech from the dock, saying that he wanted South Africa to become a truly free and open society. He wanted to live to see this come about, but, if necessary, he would die to help bring it about. He and the other defendants decided not to seek any appeal of the final verdict: They would take what came.

Mandela and his codefendants were sentenced to life imprisonment rather than death. They were taken to Robben Island, a bleak, wind-swept place just off Cape Town. This was the beginning of the 27 years Mandela would spend in prison.

When Tutu returned to South Africa in 1966, he found that most of the former leaders of the black liberation movement were dead, in jail, or in exile. This was a grim time for those who strove for racial equality.

black students. The young Nelson Mandela had studied there, as had Walter Sisulu. By the time Desmond Tutu arrived, the white government had cracked down on the University College, and the student body felt increasingly oppressed by the administration.

Desmond Tutu had always been an optimist. Throughout his life, he had overcome many difficulties, ranging from poverty to tuberculosis. He sought to bring the spirit of hope to a younger generation of black South Africans, but he found that many were increasingly bitter and thought violence was a proper response to the policies of apartheid. To persuade them otherwise would become one of the great causes of Desmond Tutu's life.

Some people have accused Desmond Tutu of hypocrisy because he sent his four children to schools outside of South Africa. The Tutus made this decision during their time in Alice. Desmond and Leah had seen the wonderful effects of a British education on their children, and they remembered well the segregated system that Tutu had fled during the 1950s. So he and Leah sent their four children to different schools in different lands. Tutu never answered the charges of being a hypocrite. To him it was obvious that he must seek the best for his children, while the same time he worked for the good of all black South Africans. Indeed, it was around this time that he started talking about the need to work for the future of all South Africans, regardless of skin color.

To some extent, Tutu was working against the grain. The late 1960s were a time of a rising black consciousness in South Africa, and many blacks did not want to hold out any well-being or friendship toward whites. Though this was never Desmond Tutu's approach, he was still able to befriend many leaders in the Black Consciousness Movement, one of them being Steven Biko.

Born in the townships, Steven Biko had managed to attend college, where he had become a leader for black South Africans. He spoke of pride in being black, the beauty of being black, and the need for South Africans to embrace their tribal heritage. At first there was no room for whites in this dream of Steven Biko's, but he changed over time.

Along with being called a hypocrite, Desmond Tutu has also been charged with being a job jumper. He seldom stayed in one position for more than three years, and he often left jobs other people would have considered plum assignments. So it was with his position at Alice.

CHAPTER 4

The Crisis Comes

Tutu left South Africa to become a lecturer at the University of Botswana, in the mountain kingdom of Lesotho. Few Americans today know much about Lesotho or can even place it on a map. It is interesting geographically because it is the only country in the world in which all its terrain lies higher than 5,000 feet above sea level. The kingdom of Lesotho has long been separate from the State of South Africa, and the British who had once ruled the area treated the two peoples differently. South Africa became a unified commonwealth in 1910, and the kingdom of Lesotho attained its independence from Great Britain in 1967. The Tutus went to Lesotho in 1970.

Lesotho was a precious breath of fresh air, because apartheid was not practiced there. There were aspects of the kingdom that reminded Desmond Tutu of Great Britain, and there were also parts of the landscape that very much reminded him of South Africa. In many ways this was the perfect compromise for him, and it was good for his family as well.

The Tutu children were all in private boarding schools at this time, and it was easier for their parents to reach them while they were living in Lesotho. Desmond Tutu also found greater freedom in Lesotho; racial prejudice was less evident here. As for being a university lecturer, this was something for which Desmond Tutu was particularly well-suited. He lectured on Old Testament and New Testament theology and enjoyed an excellent relationship with his students. Living in Lesotho allowed him to become more athletic, as well; Tutu did some mountain climbing and felt the fresh air improved his health.

At the same time, Desmond and Leah were very conscious that things were going badly for their compatriots in South Africa. Apartheid was stronger than ever. In fact, the white minority government of South Africa had designed a new plan called "grand apartheid." Petty apartheid, which had begun in 1948, was bad enough. Petty apartheid meant that whites, blacks, coloreds, and Indians were separated in the cities where they met. It also meant blacks had to live in separate townships—they could not live in suburbs or the major cities. At least petty apartheid, though, had allowed for the possibility of blacks to live in urban areas. Grand apartheid, designed by Hendrik Verwoerd in the mid-1950s, was beginning to be realized in the late 1960s. By enforcing this policy, the government intended to remove all black South Africans to their tribal homelands and keep them there. Eventually, 80 percent of the South African population would be forced onto roughly 13 percent of the land. The white South African government then announced that blacks would lose their South African citizenship as they were absorbed into the new tribal homelands. Desmond Tutu watched all this from the sidelines. He was anxious and concerned, but he had not yet found the right venue for protesting these changes.

RETURNING TO LONDON

In 1972, Desmond Tutu was offered the position of associate director of the Theological Education Fund, run by the Anglican Church. This was a great honor, but he could not fulfill its tasks while remaining in Lesotho. Therefore, he made the difficult decision to pick up yet again and move with his family back to Great Britain. On a cold winter day in 1973, the Tutus arrived in England for the second time. They soon remembered why they had loved this land so much in the first place.

The new job was nearly perfect for Desmond Tutu. It involved a lot of traveling and a lot of time spent in foreign nations, including some that had recently won independence from their colonial rulers. By traveling to nations in Africa and the Middle East, Desmond Tutu gained more hope for the future of his own homeland. Surely, it would only be a matter of time before South Africans achieved what Rhodesians, Libyans, Iraqis, and Egyptians had done before.

There were controversies, however. Desmond Tutu had a wonderful way of reaching out to people and his staff and making them feel loved, but he was rather poor at keeping financial accounts. He was never accused of misuse of funds, but there were financial irregularities. Whenever he was called to account for these, Tutu pleaded his ignorance on financial matters and pledged to do better in the future. Because of his exceptional ability in fund-raising, and in raising awareness throughout the Anglican world, he continued in the position for some time.

Early in 1975, the wheel of fortune turned yet again. Desmond Tutu learned that the archbishop of Johannesburg, South Africa, had died, and a major decision needed to be made about his replacement. Some people suggested that Desmond Tutu should become the new archbishop, but he felt this was beyond his capability at the time. A halfhearted attempt was made at his candidacy, but this fell short, and another man was chosen to be the new archbishop. That was fine with Tutu. Just a few days later, however, he learned that the new bishop had asked him to become the new dean of Johannesburg, the second-highest appointment in that diocese in the Anglican system.

Desmond Tutu faced a tough choice once again. He was quite happy directing the Theological Fund, and his family members were delighted to be living in England. Desmond and Leah were both thrilled that they had the ability to vote for the first time in their lives. Leah was especially happy to be living in England and thought it was much better for their children.

Throughout his life, Desmond Tutu relied more on spiritual strength than human will. He may have wanted to stay in England, but he felt called to this new position; after some meditation and prayer, he decided to accept. The Tutus packed their bags once more and soon arrived back in their homeland.

JOURNEY TO JO'BURG

Desmond Tutu had grown up in the neighborhoods around Johannesburg, but he had been a street urchin, and now he returned as the illustrious dean of the archdiocese. He could very well have taken advantage of the benefits afforded by his new station, but he and Leah made a conscious choice not to separate themselves from their compatriots. The couple chose to live in the black township of Orlando, part of the greater conglomeration of Soweto. One of their close neighbors, in both proximity and friendship, was Winnie Mandela. The wife of Nelson Mandela, she had spent the last 10 years living as a single woman because her husband was in jail on Robben Island, off the coast of South Africa. Winnie was a large, boisterous, exuberant woman who had become something like the mother of the black nation in her husband's absence. She became a great friend of the Tutus.

Desmond Tutu had never known Nelson Mandela in earlier years, but he was a great admirer of Mandela in the present. Like many black South Africans, Tutu saw Mandela as the strength and spirit of the black nation. Over the next decade, Tutu would make many efforts and lead many protests to seek Mandela's release. His old friend and mentor, Father Trevor Huddleston, would do similar things in Great Britain during those years. For the moment, though, Desmond Tutu had to grow into his new responsibilities as dean of Johannesburg.

He thrived in his new post. He loved ministering to his flock. The number of congregants increased, despite the fact that a few white parishioners decided they really could not accept a black man as their spiritual leader. Tutu enjoyed excellent relations with his boss, the archbishop of Johannesburg. All was well in his personal life, and his professional life was thriving, but now a crisis came in the affairs of the nation.

RIOTS AND MURDER

The terrible Soweto riots began on June 16, 1976. We have already seen how the student protests against the teaching of the Dutch language Afrikaans led to violence and mayhem. Tutu was not on hand at the beginning, but he appeared on the scene as soon as he could. Weeping and dramatically upset, he called on both sides to back off and keep the peace. It was not to be. As Desmond Tutu had written in his letter to Prime Minister John Vorster, a people can take so much and no more. Black South Africans had reached a breaking point.

A state of emergency was declared. Military troops and police kept guard on the black townships around Johannesburg, but the riots continued, albeit at a slower pace. Within the next six months, about 500 people were killed in and around Johannesburg. Most of them were children or teenagers.

Public opinion around the world began to turn against the white South African government. Sanctions were not yet imposed, but discussion of them increased, and the United Nations issued strong statements about the abuse of human rights. Even so, the white minority government stood firm. Desmond Tutu was no longer in South Africa, however. For the second time in his career, he had left his homeland for Lesotho.

BISHOP OF LESOTHO

Being dean of Johannesburg had been impressive enough. Now Tutu was called to an even higher office: bishop of Lesotho. Desmond and Leah moved back to Lesotho. Their children were now older, and one or two were in their early college years. One daughter would later become an Anglican priest.

Desmond Tutu's enthronement as bishop of Lesotho was, to this point, the most glorious moment of his life. Many friends and relatives were there to congratulate him; he was the first black person to reach such a status either in South Africa or Lesotho. One of the people he would most like to have seen was not present, though: The white South African government refused Father Trevor Huddleston a visa to pass through its borders. So, Father Huddleston conducted a special ceremony at Saint Paul's Cathedral in London to commemorate the elevation of his old friend.

Lesotho was a happy place for the Tutus. Tutu thrived in his new capacity as bishop. He traveled around the country regularly, often on horseback, and came to know all the priests of his diocese. Some people marvel at his remarkable memory, but Desmond Tutu insists that a man of God must come to know his flock one by one and name by name. He was in the midst of developing his personal theory of theology, one he calls *Ubuntu* ("brotherhood"). The theory is quite simple: "A person is a person *through* other persons."[16] Many South African tribal peoples spoke (and speak) of Ubuntu as the highest form of social good. If a person shows strong social skills and interest in his fellow human beings, then he is called a person with high Ubuntu, which is a great compliment.

Desmond Tutu wrote many books, but much of his theology comes from the oral tradition, in his sermons and speeches. He developed his idea of Ubuntu theology to the point where he spoke of it regularly; it became the basis of his personal ministry. According to this belief, people cannot develop on their own. Everyone is dependent, in that he or she has benefited from the presence, actions, or prayers of many other people. No baby grows to become a child, much less an adult, without a great deal of help. No adult man or woman becomes the best person he or she can without the counsel and assistance of others. Tutu became fond of delivering this anecdote to illustrate the concept:

> I once went to a garden party in England in the early seventies. I don't know why, but we were expected to pay for our own tea. I offered to do so for an acquaintance I met there. Now he could have said, "No, thank you," and I would have understood. But you could have knocked me down with a feather when he replied, "No, I won't be subsidized." Well, I never. As if we were not all subsidized, not only by all those whose graciousness and gifts have allowed us to become who we are but also by the grace and gifts that God has given us.[17]

Traveling about Lesotho on horseback, Tutu was very happy. He was constantly aware of what was happening in his South African homeland, just across the border, however. For that country, 1977 proved even worse than 1976.

STEVEN BIKO

When Nelson Mandela and Walter Sisulu (both prominent leaders of the African National Congress) went to prison on Robben Island in 1964, black South Africans were bereft of leadership for several years. Their strong young men were gone, locked up on a prison island. It turned out the white minority government made a mistake in keeping men like Mandela and Sisulu together, where they could communicate, but this was not known for some time to come.

At the start of the 1970s, a new group of much younger leaders began to emerge. One of the most prominent was Steven Biko, whose story was later commemorated in the film *Cry Freedom*. In his mid twenties, Steven Biko began teaching about Black

Steven Biko (above) began teaching about Black Pride, or Black Consciousness, in South Africa in the 1970s. Biko was severely restricted in his freedom to travel or speak by the South African government, but he found ways around the rules. In 1977, however, he was arrested on charges of subversion and died after suffering brutality at the hands of the police.

Pride or Black Consciousness. A similar movement had begun in the United States a few years later, but the two groups were essentially unconnected. Steven Biko came to the decision on his own that blacks are worthy and beautiful in all ways. At first he taught a reverse form of racism, saying that blacks were better than whites, but one or two new white friends managed to change his opinion. One of these was the renowned South African journalist Donald Woods.

Steven Biko spent several years under severe pass law restrictions. This meant he could not speak in public; in fact, he could not speak to more than one person at a time without breaking the law. Biko found many ways around the rules and

Cry Freedom

Richard Attenborough's powerful film *Cry Freedom* was released in 1987, a time when Americans were becoming more aware of the evils of apartheid.

The film depicts the growth of friendship between the white South African journalist Donald Woods and the black activist Steven Biko (portrayed by Denzel Washington). Woods interviewed Biko, thinking it would be a swift journalistic assignment, but having met Biko and experienced the living conditions of Soweto, Donald Woods became a changed man. He began to help Biko in any way he could, including, at times, sheltering Biko's family.

Biko was detained, arrested, and tortured in a series of horrific events that have come to symbolize the South African police state at its worst. He died after being placed in the back of a police van and being transported on a 600-mile trip.

Donald Woods later came under suspicion by the white South African government. He and his family made a daring escape to Lesotho, then flew over South African territory to reach freedom in Botswana. Their story is poignant in that they were members of the elite white South African establishment, yet after challenging the government, even they had to flee for their lives.

laws, but, in 1977, he was finally charged with subversion against the state. Interrogated and beaten, he was near death when the police put him in the back seat of a police van and drove him 600 miles (965 kilometers) to Pretoria. This rough ride accomplished what direct beating and torture had not.

There were probably many deaths like that of Steven Biko that were hushed up by the authorities. Because of his many friends, and especially the reporting of journalist Donald Woods, though, Biko's story became common knowledge around the world. The white South African government vehemently denied the story at first, but as the facts came out, it turned from denial to defiance. The minister of justice, Jimmy Kruger, declared in public, "Biko's death leaves me cold."[18]

THE FUNERAL OF STEVEN BIKO

Desmond Tutu left Lesotho for a few days to be present at Steven Biko's funeral. Even though he was out of his homeland most of the time, many black South Africans saw him as a natural leader, and he was one of several speakers at the funeral, which was attended by about 20,000 people. In his speech, he said,

> When we heard the news "Steve Biko is dead" we were struck numb with disbelief. No, it can't be true! No, it must be a horrible nightmare and we will awake and find that really it is different—that Steve is alive even if it be in detention. But no, dear friends, he is dead and we are still numb with pain and grief and groan with anguish, "Oh, God, where are you? Oh, God, do you really care? How can you let this happen to us?"[19]

This was exactly the type of moment that Desmond Tutu's Ubuntu theology had prepared him for. Because of his deep belief in a loving God and a merciful one, Tutu was able to offer hope to those who listened that day:

We weep with and pray for Ntsiki [Mrs. Biko] and all of Steve's family. We weep for ourselves. But that can't be the end of the story, because despite all that points to the contrary, God cares. He cares about right and wrong. He cares about oppression and injustice. He cares about bulldozers and detentions without trial. And so, paradoxically, we give thanks for Steve and for his life and his death.[20]

Tutu concluded:

If God is on our side, who can be against us? What can separate us from the love of Christ? Can affliction or hardship? Can persecution, hunger, nakedness, peril, or the sword? We are being done to death for thy sake all day long, as the scripture says; we are being treated like sheep for slaughter—and yet in spite of all, overwhelming victory is ours through him who loves us.[21]

Of course, not all who listened agreed with what they heard. Some were furious, accusing Desmond Tutu of being an appeaser. A majority of those who listened, though, understood Desmond Tutu's call for grief rather than revenge. Although Tutu went back to Lesotho after the funeral, he could see that God was calling him back to his troubled homeland.

CHAPTER 5

Archbishop of Johannesburg

Desmond Tutu was asked to become the general secretary of the South African Council of Churches (SACC) in 1977, the year Steven Biko died. Once again he was called away from a position of high responsibility to an even greater one. Some people resented Desmond Tutu's leaving the kingdom of Lesotho (he had been there only a little over a year), but Tutu's good friends gave him their full confidence, saying that he had been called again and that God was directing his action:

> But what He had in mind was that you should make it possible for
> a Mosotho of the Basotho to be made ready for the office and work
> of a Bishop in the Church of God here! So I hope you feel you can
> say *Nunc Dimitis*, as far as Lesotho is concerned, in great peace
> and thankfulness.[22]

Tutu started his new job in March 1978. As general secretary of the South African Council of Churches, he was now an administrator

Bishop Desmond Tutu is pictured above in 1981, when he was the general secretary of the South African Council of Churches, a position he had been appointed to in 1978. In this job, Tutu was more of an administrator than a priest, though he still found time to preach from time to time.

rather than a priest. Tutu still found time to preach occasionally, but the council took up an increasing amount of his time.

The South African Council of Churches had been established in the 1940s. The intention had been for all churches within South Africa—Protestant, Catholic, and other—to be united in one general body. This had been the case for some years, but when the council strongly criticized apartheid, the Dutch Reformed Church removed itself from the organization, lessening the universal quality of that body.

Tutu viewed his new job as a parish without frontiers. He longed for the day when all South Africans would see each other as equals and brothers. While working toward that goal, he had a very informal and relaxed relationship with most of his staff. He had two secretaries: one black and one white. The two adored him equally, and the office was often filled with laughter.

As when he had been president of the Theological Fund, Tutu had plenty of reasons to travel in his new job. Most of his travel was within South Africa itself, however, because the white South African government was reluctant to allow him to use his passport to go elsewhere. Until about 1977, the year of Steven Biko's funeral, Desmond Tutu had been seen as a gadfly at most, not very important as far as the government was concerned. His strong words at that funeral—he had compared Steven Biko to Christ—and his new high position as general secretary, though, focused more of the government's attention upon him. Perhaps he was not in danger of assassination or abduction, but the government would use any opportunity it had to thwart his purposes. White South Africans as a whole had become more aware of him. On one occasion, as Tutu went through an airport, he distinctly heard a white woman say, "Isn't that that bastard Tutu?—If I had a gun, I would shoot him now."[23]

Threats like this did not deter Desmond Tutu. He was fortified by his faith and by the importance of the task at hand. He prayed and meditated regularly, and he was strengthened by his ever-faithful wife. One of his biographers, Shirley Du Boulay, wrote of Tutu,

> His life is shot through with prayer. He rises early in the morning, sometimes as early as 3:30, to be sure of a full hours' prayer before his daily jog; then, after a quick breakfast, he goes to mass or, if it is not possible to go to church, he celebrates at home, with Leah as his single congregant. During the working day every interview in meeting is preceded by a short prayer.[24]

FINANCIAL DIFFICULTIES

Desmond Tutu was never very good with money. In his youth, his parents had so little money that whatever they had, they spent. Tutu's life was more blessed in that he had lots of money pass through his hands, but he seldom kept a close watch on it. He never had much trouble with his personal or family finances, but the council came under increasing scrutiny in the early 1980s. Tutu was very aware of the danger. If he and the council could not be trusted with large funds, then their message would be ignored by the larger public. Therefore, Tutu decided to lay all the books open to the public and to allow a full-scale investigation to take place. This was a good decision, but it led to plenty of difficulties.

The investigation practically spawned a scandal. Tutu was never accused of diverting funds for himself or friends, but the books were kept in a very irregular manner. The white South African newspapers pounced on this opportunity to embarrass Tutu, and they often succeeded. On one occasion, the newspapers lambasted him for rubbing his hands together as if in glee; he had to go to great lengths to explain he did this to comfort the hand that had been withered since his severe bout with tuberculosis.

The investigation took nearly two years. Tutu and all leading members of the SACC were cleared of any wrongdoing, but the entire affair had been an embarrassment to the organization. Tutu and his colleagues vowed nothing of the sort would ever take place again. When he later ran the Truth and Reconciliation Commission (TRC), Tutu was extremely vigilant about the financial records and the need to keep them transparent (able to be viewed by anyone).

During 1981 and 1982, while Tutu was taken up with the matter of financial concerns, race relations in South Africa grew even worse. Tutu and other South Africans were very disappointed by the change in administrations in the United States. They had favored the administration of then-President Jimmy Carter, but he was not re-elected. Ronald Reagan took office in 1981.

THE "GREAT CROCODILE"

In South Africa, there was a new prime minister to deal with. John Vorster was out of office; he had been replaced by P.W. Botha (pronounced "Vota"). A tall, imposing man called the "Great Crocodile" by some of his colleagues, Botha wanted no compromise with the black majority. During the early 1980s, he was most concerned with building up the South African military. South Africa had good trade and economic relations with the United States and Israel, and both countries sold many guns, helicopters, and tanks to South Africa.

Tutu viewed this military buildup with alarm. He did all he could, sending letters first to Prime Minister John Vorster and now to P.W. Botha. Because neither man would respond or make any changes, Tutu stepped up his international profile, seeking to bring pressure on the white South African government.

The early 1980s were a rather grim time in international affairs. The United States was preoccupied with a hostage crisis in Iran. The Soviet Union had invaded Afghanistan. Many Western powers, including Britain, were mired in deep economic recessions. Yet in the midst of all this, there was hope. A handful of dedicated men and women were bringing abuses of human rights to the forefront. Desmond Tutu was one such man. Another was Terry Waite, the personal representative of the archbishop of Canterbury. On another level, there were people like Mother Teresa, who called worldwide attention to the plight of the poor. It was the age of television and international media as a whole, though, that made the troubles of many people, including black South Africans, more visible.

Despite the surge in awareness, little progress was made at first. Repressive regimes continued throughout much of the developing world. Russia and the United States continued their Cold War dance of "Mutual Assured Destruction," meaning that both sides knew that to launch a nuclear attack would mean the end of both nations—and perhaps the entire world.

1984

The year 1984 proved to be a decisive break in the struggles of that decade. In the 1930s, George Orwell had used *1984* as the title of his futuristic novel, suggesting that governments would use television and other media to run the lives of their citizens. "Big Brother" would watch from afar, and everyone would be suspect. Some people believed that *1984* had truly foretold the future, and that the world was beginning to resemble George Orwell's nightmarish vision.

As it turned out, the autumn of 1984 was one of the most dramatic and frightening times the world had seen for many years. In October, a chemical plant owned by the American company Union Carbide exploded in Bhopal, India. Thousands of people were killed, either immediately or through the slow death of chemical poisoning. Just a month later, the prime minister of India, Indira Gandhi, was assassinated by one of her Sikh bodyguards after she had ordered an attack on the Sikhs' holiest shrine, the Golden Temple in Amritsar. Things looked grim indeed.

The leader of the Soviet Union, Yuri Andropov, was almost completely unknown. For more than a decade previously, there had been the stable, though repressive, government of Leonid Brezhnev. Now there was great concern about what might happen between Russia and the United States. American President Ronald Reagan had called the Soviet Union an "evil empire," further poisoning relations between the two countries.

In the midst of all this, South Africa was about to explode. New riots broke out in the summer of 1984. Eight years had passed since the Soweto riots, and things only seemed to be getting worse. Several new tribal homelands had been created. The blacks who lived there forfeited their South African citizenship, but many tribal leaders felt this was a worthy exchange. Tutu and other black liberation leaders denounced it as a sell-out of black interests. Not surprisingly, Tutu won the enmity of several tribal chieftains, one of whom was Mangosuthu Buthelezi, a Zulu chieftain. A new state of emergency was declared in the summer of 1984. Just when everything seemed to be at its worst, though, Desmond Tutu received some genuinely good news.

THE NOBEL PEACE PRIZE

Created in 1896, the Nobel Peace Prize had been awarded to 68 individuals over the years, and to a handful of organizations, as well. Bishop Desmond Tutu of South Africa was the sixty-ninth person to receive the award, and the second South African. His predecessor was Albert Luthuli, leader of the African National Congress, who had won the 1960 Nobel Peace Prize. Luthuli's selection had been a milestone, for he was the first African, and only the second non-European, to receive the award. Now, in 1984, it was Desmond Tutu's turn.

Tutu was in New York City, teaching for a semester at the General Theological Seminary, when he was informed of the honor. Delighted with the news, he announced his intention to visit his homeland before going to Norway to receive the Peace Prize. Within a matter of days, Tutu and Leah were in Cape Town,

South Africa. The white government of South Africa did its best to ignore its famous citizen; some government leaders expressed irritation that the Peace Prize had gone to a rabble-rousing priest,

History of the Nobel Peace Prize

Alfred Nobel died on December 10, 1896. His will directed that the vast majority of his fortune—estimated at nine million dollars—was to be used for the establishment and award of annual prizes in five categories: literature, medicine or physiology, chemistry, physics, and for the "person who had made the greatest contribution to the cause of promoting friendship among nations, disarmament or limitation of armaments, as well as to the establishment and popularization of the Congresses of Peace."*

Ever since, people have marveled at the incongruity between the man, his career, and the award that was named for him. Alfred Nobel was a Swede who spent many years living in other nations; he spent a lot of time in Paris; and he died in Italy. He made his fortune in his thirties, by perfecting a process for the making of explosives, which he patented in 1867; this was the beginning of dynamite. How strange that such a man would leave most of his vast fortune to the establishment of international prizes, and that one of them would be the "Peace Prize."

The first Nobel Prizes were awarded in 1901. Nobel had established the selection process. For the Peace Prize, a committee of five people chosen by the Norwegian Parliament selects the laureates. They began a custom of announcing the prizes in October and giving the actual award on December 10 of each year, the day of Nobel's death.

More that 100 persons and organizations have been awarded the Nobel Peace Prize; Nobel's will provided that the award could be given to as many as three persons in one year. There have been numerous occasions on which it was given to two persons, and one occasion when it went to three. Examining the list of the recipients indicates that the Nobel Prize committees have indeed fulfilled Nobel's intention that the prize should not

which was what they considered him. Overall, the journey home was a bit of a disappointment; Desmond Tutu remained very much a prophet without honor in his homeland. Returning to

be limited to one national or ethnic group, but an examination also shows that there have not been many females selected for the honor (the first woman to receive the prize was Baroness Bertha von Suttner, in 1905).

Americans have fared well in the Nobel Peace Prize selection process. President Theodore Roosevelt won the award for mediating the peace conference that ended the Russo–Japanese War; President Woodrow Wilson won it for his work at the peace conference that ended World War I. But there have been some controversial selections, including that of Dr. Henry Kissinger, who, as secretary of state, worked toward ending the U.S. presence in South Vietnam (Kissinger's critics claimed it was a farce for this man, who had been behind so much of American policy that led to the Vietnam War, to receive the Peace Prize).

Two of the biggest events surrounding the Nobel Peace Prize had to do with Middle Eastern diplomacy. In 1979, Israeli Prime Minister Menachem Begin and Egyptian President Anwar Sadat shared the prize for their work in creating the Camp David Accords, a plan for peace between their two nations. In 1993, Yitzhak Rabin and Shimon Peres, both of Israel, shared the Nobel Peace Prize with Yasir Arafat; the three men had worked on the Oslo Accords, a peace agreement between Israel and the Palestinian Authority (sadly, this set of accords did not deliver on its promise).

Would Alfred Nobel have been satisfied? This is difficult to say, but, as even some critics acknowledge, it is better to light one candle than to curse the darkness. Nobel started the process in 1896, and it has been continued by presidents, prime ministers, social workers, medical doctors, and others.

---

*Irwin Adams, *The Nobel Prize*. Boston: G.K. Hall & Co., 1988, p. 193.

New York City, he was showered with awards and celebrations. The clamor became so large that even President Ronald Reagan invited Desmond Tutu for a White House visit on December 7, 1984. This was the forty-third anniversary of the Japanese attack on Pearl Harbor, but neither man had that in mind as he sat down with the other. Rather, both men were interested in the present and what might be accomplished concerning American relations with South Africa.

Tutu hoped President Reagan would put economic pressure on South Africa. Many American firms did business in South Africa, and even a limited trade boycott might force the white South African government to relax its policy of apartheid. President Reagan wanted and needed to keep South Africa on his side, however. The Cold War between the capitalist United States and the Communist Soviet Union was at one of its chilliest moments. President Reagan believed he could rely on the white South African government as a strong ally, and he was therefore reluctant to do anything to upset that relationship.

If there was anything Tutu could use to shock or surprise the American president, it was his passport. The South African government was very sparing with passports issued to blacks, and very suspicious of Tutu's globetrotting style. Tutu showed President Reagan his passport, which, under the section for listing one's nationality, read "Undeterminable at Present." This did not mean the South African government could not figure out Tutu's citizenship, but rather signaled the intention of the government to revoke the citizenship of *all* South African blacks once they had been removed to their tribal homelands. Tutu came away from this meeting disappointed. He told the press he and the president a fine conversation, but that neither had been able to convince the other of his point of view.

Tutu set off for Oslo, Norway. He took nearly 40 people with him—he wanted to emphasize that the award was being given to all who struggled against the evils of apartheid. Naturally, there were some critics who accused him of grandstanding, but this charge had become so common that Tutu just shrugged it off.

Tutu received the Nobel Peace Prize on December 10, 1984. Just minutes after the document and the $181,000 check were placed in his hands, there was a bomb threat and the room had to be cleared. For the next hour or so, Tutu led his many friends and well-wishers in singing "We Shall Overcome," while police checked the building. No bomb was found.

The next day, December 11, Tutu gave his Nobel Peace Prize acceptance speech. Each winner made a grand statement to the world of their struggles for peace and the state of peace in the world as a whole. He began:

> Before I left South Africa, a land I love passionately, we had an emergency meeting of the executive committee of the South African Council of Churches with the leaders of our member churches. We called the meeting because of the deepening crisis in our land, which has claimed nearly two hundred lives this year alone.[25]

Apartheid had been in place since 1948, and there had been a gathering of nonviolent resistance to it. The resistance had spiked in 1960, when many blacks had been killed at Sharpeville, and again in 1976 with the Soweto riots. Now the violence seemed ready to escalate once more.

Desmond Tutu was committed to a path of nonviolent resistance. He did not advocate the use of guns, bombs, or explosives. He was outraged, however, by the injustice in his homeland: "They have taken 87 percent of the land, though being only about 20 percent of our population. The rest have to make do with the remaining 13 percent. Apartheid has decreed the politics of exclusion."[26]

Tutu looked at a system that was bad enough already and threatened to become even worse:

Apartheid is upheld by a phalanx of iniquitous laws, such as the Population Registration Act, which decrees that all South Africans must be classified ethnically and duly registered according to these race categories. Many times, in the same family, one child has been classified white while another with a slightly darker hue had been classified Colored, with all the horrible consequences for the latter of being shut out from membership of a greatly privileged caste. There have, as a result, been several child suicides. This is too high a price to pay for racial purity, for it is doubtful whether any end, however desirable, can justify such a means.[27]

The system of registration was destructive indeed. In some cases, government officials entered private homes and demanded to examine each person. The notorious "pencil test" required that a pencil be inserted in the hair and the person had to move his or her head rapidly. If the pencil stayed in the hair, the person was designated black or Native. If the pencil fell out, the person would be classified white, Indian, or colored.

Desmond Tutu had always been known for his good spirit and humor. He amused his audience by recounting the following anecdote:

Once a Zambian and a South African, it is said, were talking. The Zambian boasted about their Minister of Naval Affairs. The South African asked, 'But you have no navy, no access to the sea. How then can you have a Minister of Naval Affairs?' The Zambian retorted: "Well, in South Africa you have a Minister of Justice, don't you?"[28]

Though South Africa was his greatest concern, Desmond Tutu spoke also of other parts of the world. He pointed to the repressive regimes in Latin America and other parts of Africa, in the Philippines, and elsewhere. He saved some of his strongest words, however, for the capitalist West:

American-South African Relations

Until about 1950, South Africa's primary relationship with the Western world had been through Great Britain. Around that time, the United States replaced Britain as the major Western superpower, however, and from then on, Pretoria's relationship with Washington, D.C., became more important than its relationship with London.

President Dwight Eisenhower was the first American leader to really become aware of racial troubles in South Africa. He had plenty of his own such problems at home, though; this period marked the early stages of the civil rights movement in the United States. For that reason, Eisenhower decided that he would not comment on events 6,000 miles away.

American presidents from John Kennedy to Richard Nixon did not concern themselves with South Africa. In the 1970s, Russia was strong and becoming increasingly belligerent, however, so presidents Gerald Ford and Jimmy Carter had to be concerned with Soviet incursions into Africa. Gerald Ford was a strong ally of the white South African government, but Jimmy Carter took several opportunities to criticize apartheid and human rights violations in that country. Desmond Tutu and other black South Africans were cheered by Jimmy Carter's approach, but they were dismayed when Ronald Reagan took office in 1981.

Reagan was a true Cold War warrior. He saw the contest between the United States and the Soviet Union as the great issue of the time. Therefore, as long as the white South African government proved itself a firm ally in the struggle against Communism, Ronald Reagan would be an ally of that government and would not condemn apartheid.

Many American citizens were angry about what was happening in South Africa. They implored the United States government to create economic sanctions against the white minority government in that land. All such efforts failed, though, as long as Ronald Reagan believed he had a firm ally in Pretoria.

Because there is global insecurity, nations are engaged in a mad arms race, spending billions of dollars wastefully on instruments of destruction, when millions are starving. And yet, just a fraction of what is expended so obscenely on defense budgets would make the difference in enabling God's children to fill their stomachs, be educated and given the chance to lead fulfilled and happy lives.[29]

Everyone in the room knew this was true. The United States and Soviet Union spent more money on Cold War armaments, including nuclear weapons, than on the fulfillment of human needs. Both Russia and the United States claimed that once their respective nations won the Cold War, they would be able to help the hungry, oppressed peoples of the world. Desmond Tutu was one of many, however, who said: Enough! The time had come now.

Tutu concluded his acceptance speech with a call for peace, justice, and reconciliation: "Let us work to be peacemakers, those given a wonderful share in our Lord's ministry of reconciliation. If we want peace, so we have been told, let us work for justice. Let us beat our swords into plowshares."[30] His speech was over, but his work continued.

CHAPTER 6

The Dark
Before the
Dawn

Winning the Nobel Peace Prize was a great achievement for Desmond Tutu. For him, something had changed in the great struggle, and things would never look so bad again. This was not true for many of his fellow black South Africans, however; the way they saw things, their situation was only getting worse.

The white minority government of South Africa refused to acknowledge Desmond Tutu's achievement. Public officials either gave a terse "no comment" on the matter or criticized this man who, in their view, had brought so much trouble to his country. Meanwhile, the white South African minority continued its repressive form of government.

Despite his earlier reluctance, President Ronald Reagan went so far as to criticize the white South African government in his speech on International Freedom Day. His speech was on December 10, 1984, the same day that Desmond Tutu received the Nobel Peace Prize in Norway. This new public attention did not dismay the white South African government, though; on the contrary, its leaders announced their intention to be guided by their conscience, not by what the international community said.

There were, however, new honors for Desmond Tutu. In 1985, Tutu was chosen to be the new Anglican bishop of Johannesburg. He was delighted with his selection. Preparations were made for his installation, which was scheduled for winter 1986. By now,

Albert Luthuli

Albert Luthuli, shown in this 1961 picture, was the first African to win the Nobel Peace Prize, and the first black person of any continent to do so. As the president of the African National Congress, Luthuli's movements were severely restricted by the South African government, which refused to permit him to travel to Oslo to officially receive the prize.

Albert Luthuli was the first African to win the Nobel Peace Prize and the first black person from any continent to do so.

A Zulu tribal chief, Luthuli grew up in the eastern part of South Africa, the son of a Methodist missionary. He received a better education than was typical for blacks of the time, and he thrived during the 1920s and 1930s, when most black South Africans were declining in status.

Sometime in the 1940s, Luthuli changed his life, leaving his role as tribal leader to become an outspoken member of the African National Congress. He participated in many of the protest movements of the 1940s and early 1950s, and in 1956 he became

Tutu had become such a well-known international figure that many leading dignitaries wanted to come to his installation. Coretta Scott King, the widow of Martin Luther King, Jr., came, as did Senator Edward Kennedy of Massachusetts, and many other liberal and Democratic leaders from the United States and Western Europe.

president of the ANC. In this position he became good friends and close allies with Nelson Mandela, Walter Sisulu, and others.

The white South African government punished Luthuli by confining him to his tribal ranch. Under the pass laws, he could not hold any meetings, or even speak to more than one person at a time. Luthuli kept his composure remarkably well. He worked on his major literary effort, *Let My People Go*, which was published in 1962. He wrote:

> It is a tragedy that the great majority of South African whites are determined to permit no peaceful evolution. They have for so long refused to adapt themselves, and insisted that all adaptation shall come from us, that they seem incapable now of anything but rigidity. . . . Each new challenge leads to a further hardening of heart.*

Luthuli continued to call for peaceful means in the struggle for black freedom, and in 1963 he was awarded the Nobel Peace Prize. He was not able to go to Oslo, Norway, to accept the award, though, because the South African government neither relaxed his confinement nor issued him a passport. The first black person ever to win this prestigious prize was unable to celebrate it in the proper way.

Luthuli died at home in 1968. By then, Martin Luther King Jr. had won the Nobel Peace Prize, the second black person to do so. Desmond Tutu was the third.

---

*Albert Luthuli, *Let My People Go*. New York: McGraw-Hill, 1962, p. 209.

Tutu was now the spiritual leader of a diocese with 105 churches and 100,000 parishioners. About half those churches were exclusively white and had been as long as they existed. Tutu could not change things like that overnight, as he acknowledged in his enthronement address, but he had sharp words for those who said he should stay out of politics:

> We are accused of mixing politics with religion. . . . I have kept saying that what we do or say is based on our understanding of the biblical imperatives and the Gospel of Jesus Christ. The God of the Bible is first encountered not in a religious setting, but in an out-and-out political experience, in helping a rabble of slaves to escape from bondage.[31]

As usual, Tutu mixed humor with serious thoughts. He hoped his congregants would find him "not such an ogre," as they feared. Tutu's power was implicit in his message. Here he was, living in one of the most repressive regimes of his time, yet he dared talk back to the government and assert the rights of his parishioners as human beings, regardless of what the government said.

Some white parishioners chose to leave the Anglican diocese after Tutu became its bishop. They were unable to reconcile their notions of blacks as inferior with his articulate presence. Tutu had attained a pinnacle never before reached by a black South African; he was a figure of such international attention that even the white South African government did not dare touch him. Yet there were still problems.

Tutu risked his life on a number of occasions. As the repression continued, violence rose, and there were a number of times when Tutu ran into an angry crowd to rescue someone. The most famous case was in July 1985. Tutu was in Duduza, a township 30 miles east of Johannesburg. He led a funeral for four men recently shot and killed by the police. As the funeral ended, the crowd turned ugly. Some people claimed they had found a black man who was a police informant. The man's automobile

In 1985, violence broke out when a crowd of black South Africans attacked a suspected police informer. Desmond Tutu, who opposed violence in all forms, waded into the angry crowd in order to stop the fighting, as shown above.

was toppled on its side, then set aflame. Shouts arose from the crowd, as people prepared to "necklace" the suspected informant. (This meant that an automobile tire filled with gasoline would be placed around his neck and set afire.) Tutu rushed straight into the crowd, saying, "This undermines the struggle."[32]

Some in the crowd answered, "No, it encourages the struggle!"[33] Tutu and his aides managed to keep the crowd away, then had the man taken away in Tutu's own car. Tutu stayed and pled with the crowd, imploring them not to become bestial in the face of the bestiality that they had all suffered over the course of time. "Let us not use methods in the struggle that we will later be ashamed of."[34] Tutu certainly invited the anger, even the wrath, of his fellow blacks by defending police informers and collaborators with apartheid. Many years later, he outlined his reasons for doing so, under the overall concept of Ubuntu theology—his philosophy of brotherhood:

> Dear child of God, if we are truly to understand that God loves all of us, we must recognize that he loves our enemies, too. God does not share our hatred, no matter what the offense we have endured. We try to claim God for ourselves and for our cause, but God's love is too great to be confined to any one side of a conflict or any one religion. And our prejudices, regardless of whether they are based on religion, race, nationality, gender, sexual orientation, or anything else, are absolutely and utterly ridiculous in God's eyes.[35]

His message was not popular in the violent 1980s.

GOVERNING BY CARROT AND STICK

Prime Minister Botha was an intelligent man. He knew that blacks and whites had to come to some form of reconciliation for the nation to survive, but he could not get too far ahead of his Afrikaner voters. Very few of them wanted to create a new society in which blacks and whites would be equal. The most Botha could do was to relax some forms of apartheid. The pass laws were relaxed, and a handful of political prisoners were released. Most notably, Winnie Mandela was released from the form of political exile she had suffered for several years, which kept her in solitary confinement for long stretches of time.

Blacks continued to be segregated into the tribal homelands through enforcement of the grand apartheid policy, which at the same time deprived most of them of their South African citizenship. Worse, the gold and diamond mine owners made it a policy to hire fewer blacks and more whites for these jobs. One of the few ways that a black South African had been able to make a living was by working in the gold and diamond pits; now even this was about to be denied him.

Tutu continued to lead the fight against apartheid. He was the most visible South African person, familiar to people around the world. He yearned, however, to have comrades in this struggle. The person best suited for that was Nelson Mandela. Sent to prison in 1964, Nelson Mandela was still incarcerated. He lived under better conditions than before, having been moved from Robben Island to a more comfortable prison on the mainland. No longer was he chopping cement or limestone

Afrikaner Political Leaders

John Vorster and P.W. Botha were only two of the most extreme of the Afrikaner leaders. Afrikaner politicians in general tended to be verbose and aggressive. Perhaps this was because they remembered being an oppressed people in the past.

The Anglo-Boer War of 1899–1902 created lasting bitterness in the Afrikaner community. Even after the British and Dutch sections of South Africa were unified in 1910, many Afrikaners continued to think of the British as conquerors. Many Afrikaner politicians wanted the country to stay out of both World War I and World War II, which they saw as "British" conflicts.

Afrikaner politicians came to power in 1948 and intended to hold on to that power. One of the most articulate leaders was the minister of education, Hendrik Verwoerd, who called for the expansion of petty apartheid (the pass laws) and the creation of grand apartheid (the establishment of the tribal homelands). Verwoerd was assassinated in 1966, but his ideas remained the cornerstone of many Afrikaner beliefs.

When apartheid fell in 1990 and 1991, many Afrikaner leaders were astounded by the speed with which their world changed. Many of them sought refuge from the inevitable judgment process to follow. Some testified willingly before the Truth and Reconciliation Commission, whereas others were virtually dragged there.

blocks into little bits. Tutu stepped up his calls for the release of men like Nelson Mandela; he was joined in this by his old mentor, Father Trevor Huddleston. In 1988, Father Huddleston organized a movement in England called "Freedom at 70." Born in 1918, Nelson Mandela turned 70 in July of that year, and millions of well-wishers around the globe sent him their affection and sympathy.

Music played a large role in the cause for South African freedom. Black South Africans had always been enthusiastic musicians, whether in a professional or amateur capacity. Father Huddleston organized an eight-hour rock concert at Wembley Stadium in London, and many prominent musicians came to play for the cause. Paul Simon's music played a large role in bringing South Africa's plight to the attention of the world. Simon's album *Graceland* came out in 1987. Employing South African musicians and musical traditions, it introduced a Western audience to the sounds and themes of South African music.

One song, which appeared on a benefit album produced in the mid-1980s by Artists Against Apartheid, had the title "Ain't Gonna Play Sun City." The title referred to a resort in South Africa called Sun City that many musicians and performers chose to boycott. This venue was, in fact, a gambling resort on one of the tribal "homelands." This boycott was intended to show their opposition to South Africa and its policies of apartheid. The lyrics went,

> Relocation to phony homelands
> Separation of families I can't understand
> Twenty-three million can't vote 'cause they're black
> We're stabbing our brothers and sisters in the back,
>   I'm gonna say
> Our Government tell us "we're doing all we can"
> Constructive engagement is Ronald Reagan's plan
> Meanwhile people are dying and giving up hope
> This quiet diplomacy ain't nothing but a joke

Berliners celebrate as East Germans flood through the dismantled Berlin Wall into West Berlin on November 12, 1989. It is suspected that the fall of the wall and the disintegration of other Communist states in Eastern Europe may have contributed to the unraveling of apartheid in South Africa.

I ain't gonna play Sun City
I ain't gonna play Sun City. . . .[36]

Desmond Tutu could feel the monolith of apartheid starting to waver. Twice in the 1980s, Tutu had private meetings with P.W. Botha, and both times he came away thinking that things would soon improve. Tutu had the nerve to say to Botha that things were going his way and that Botha should come over and join the blacks while they were at the stage of winning. This seemed ridiculous on the face of it, but it indicates Tutu's overriding faith in the black cause.

No one really knows why apartheid started to unravel in 1989. One suspects that the fall of the Communist states in Eastern Europe had something to do it. People around the world witnessed the collapse of the Berlin Wall and the reuniting of East and West Germany with astonishment. If this could happen, then perhaps apartheid could be dismantled in South Africa. Even so, no one would have predicted the release of Nelson Mandela in February 1990.

THE REVOLUTIONS OF 1989

In September 1989, the international scene looked much as it had for a long time. The formidable military powers of the United States and the Soviet Union faced off across a distance of thousands of miles, with Eastern and Western Europe lodged securely between the two.

Then, in October, small revolts broke out in Poland and Czechoslovakia. Similar revolts had always been crushed in the past by a combination of Polish police and Soviet security forces. The Soviet Union seemed to be paralyzed that autumn, though; no Soviet tanks rolled west to quell the disturbances, which soon spread to East and West Germany, Hungary, and elsewhere.

Then, late in October 1989, the Berlin Wall fell. The wall had stood since 1961 as a tangible, visible reminder of the power of the Soviet Union. Now it was gone, and millions of East and West

Nelson Mandela holds hands with his wife, Winnie, the day after his release from prison, where he spent 27 years. Winnie and Desmond Tutu were among the first to greet Mandela, and he spent his first night of freedom at the residence of the Tutu family.

Germans spontaneously celebrated the ability to meet and greet one another. Again, the Soviet Union did nothing.

The revolutionary fever now spread to Czechoslovakia, Romania, and elsewhere, as one Eastern European Communist government after another was swept away by mass movements of the common people. Most of these revolutions took place with a minimum of bloodshed; only in Romania did the ironfisted Communist government put up a fight.

By Christmas Day 1989, the international scene had been transformed. Millions of people who had been under Communist domination for two generations were suddenly free. Many Eastern Europeans welcomed the opportunity of turning to democratic and capitalist reforms. People around the world rejoiced, and some of them predicted that something similar might happen in South Africa.

FREEDOM FOR MANDELA

For years, Nelson Mandela had been South Africa's number one enemy of the state. President Botha and others had resolutely refused ever to release Mandela, but under President F.W. de Klerk, this event came to pass. On a warm, sunny day in February 1990, though, Mandela left prison, where he had spent 27 years. His wife, Winnie Mandela, and Desmond Tutu were among the first to greet the hero.

Mandela had spent more than 27 years imprisoned, and it was not easy to adjust to the camera, lights, and publicity. He spent his first night of freedom with the Tutu family at Bishopscourt and gave his first press conference there the next day. Then he flew off to Johannesburg to begin his return to public life.

CHAPTER 7

The Walls Come Tumbling Down

A tremendous victory had been won. Nelson Mandela was free. Apartheid still existed, but the cracks in the system were large enough that people could see light at the end of the tunnel. No one was happier than Archbishop Desmond Tutu, who had worked so long and so hard for this to happen. Yet, there were difficulties, some of which emerged right away.

Quite a few South Africans, especially those of the younger generation, thought that both Nelson Mandela and Desmond Tutu were out of step with the times. These young South Africans grew up with violence constantly confronting them, and they thought the pacifist ideas of both the political leader Mandela and the spiritual leader Tutu inadequate for the 1990s. There was even a short time when it seemed that Mandela would not be up to his new task of leadership— as if the many years in prison had taken the best out of him. These fears proved false.

After his release, Mandela began working closely with President F.W. de Klerk. De Klerk had succeeded President P.W. Botha just before the 1990 elections. The two men maintained an outward appearance of friendship, but they were actually deeply suspicious of each other.

Desmond Tutu, for his part, was suspicious of the new black and white government. During Holy Week of 1991 he gave a sermon entitled "Something Has Gone Desperately Wrong":

> It seems as if the culture of violence is taking root in our society. We are becoming brutalized and almost anesthetized to accept what is totally unacceptable. If this kind of violence that keeps erupting at regular intervals continues, then the new South Africa may dawn—and that is doubtful—but it may dawn and there will be very few around to enjoy it; and those who survive will do so only because they are tough, on the basis of the laws of the jungle: survival of the fittest, eat or be eaten, devil take the hindmost.[37]

These were tough words coming from South Africa's highest church authority:

> Something has gone desperately wrong in the black community. We black people must of course point to all the causes of violence I have pointed out and to others that I have not referred to. But ultimately we must turn the spotlight on ourselves. We can't go on forever blaming apartheid. Of course it is responsible for a great deal of evil. But ultimately, man, we are human beings and we have proved it in the resilience we have shown in the struggle for justice.[38]

Tutu implored people on all sides of the struggle to cease violence. He appealed to the political leaders to stop quietly inciting violence. He concluded with a special prayer composed by Father Trevor Huddleston:

> God bless Africa
> Guard her children

South African President F.W. de Klerk is shown here during his opening speech in Parliament on February 1, 1991, when he announced that the remaining apartheid laws would be scrapped. De Klerk was later awarded the Nobel Peace Prize, along with Nelson Mandela, for his part in ending apartheid.

Guide her rulers
And give her peace.[39]

Only later, with the benefit of hindsight, could one see that Tutu was essentially correct. There was indeed an escalation of violence in 1990 and 1991, and much of it was instigated by the white minority government. F.W. de Klerk and other Afrikaners had not given up on their goal of keeping the blacks out of government. They were not alone in inciting violence, however. Members of the African National Congress (ANC) were also involved; many of them feared the growing power of the Zulu leader Mangosuthu Buthelezi.

TRIBAL CONFLICTS

Through most of the years of apartheid, it was clear that the great enemy was the white South African government. But as apartheid began to be dismantled in the early 1990s, serious divisions among the many black South African tribes began to surface.

Desmond Tutu had never really thought of himself as a member of a tribe. Even though his father came from one tribe and his mother from another, and there had been three languages spoken in his house, Tutu always thought of himself as a South African. Moving in the educated worlds of Johannesburg, London, and Cape Town, Tutu had easily shed what remained of his tribal identity, but this was not the case for many of his fellow black South Africans.

In 1991 and 1992, a serious conflict grew between the Xhosa-speaking tribes, led by Nelson Mandela, and the Zulu-speaking tribe, led by Chief Mangosuthu Buthelezi. There were episodes of "black-on-black" violence, where Zulus were assisted by the South African secret police in killing black South Africans from other tribes. A very difficult time followed.

Social unrest continued to grow. The violence continued, and it became difficult to trace the source. Much as they disliked one another, Nelson Mandela and F.W. de Klerk worked together, seeking to create a new government that would answer the needs of most South Africans. Desmond Tutu prayed for both men and for their efforts.

In 1992 and 1993 there were several occasions when everything could have fallen apart. Violence escalated both between blacks and whites and among blacks themselves. Tutu did not hesitate to criticize both sides in the conflict, saying that everyone must work together for peace. Stumbling blocks remained, however. The Zulu tribe as a whole opposed any new elections, and many people despaired of South Africa's future. But Nelson Mandela and F.W. de Klerk managed to continue working together, and by the beginning of 1994, they had agreed that an election would be held that April. The Zulu liberation movement, called Inkatha,

President Nelson Mandela and Archbishop Desmond Tutu embrace after Tutu administered the oath to swear Mandela in as president of South Africa. Mandela was the first black man to be elected to the office in the nation's history.

boycotted the elections until the last possible moment, but when it became apparent that the elections would take place, Buthelezi finally withdrew his opposition.

THE 1994 ELECTIONS

Things came together in the spring of 1994. An agreement was finally reached under which all South Africans would go to the polls in April to vote for a new president.

Nelson Mandela and F.W. de Klerk were the two presidential candidates. There was little doubt that Nelson Mandela would win, given the much larger black population, but there was a great deal of fear that violence would happen at the polls. As Desmond

Tutu later pointed out, it would have only taken a few men with AK-47s to kill many people and disrupt the whole voting process. Miraculously, the elections proceeded safely, and after some days of counting, the results were announced: Nelson Mandela would be president of the new South Africa.

Tutu later described the scene:

> Yes, our first election turned out to be a deeply spiritual event, a religious experience, Transfiguration experience, a mountaintop experience. We had won a spectacular victory over injustice, oppression, and evil. Friendship, laughter, joy, caring, all of these were impossible for us as one nation, and now here

Critics of the Peacemaker

There was always a powerful contradiction about Desmond Tutu. He was a bold man, given to rhetorical speeches and grand gestures, but he also dreaded criticism and opposition. Many times he freely confessed his great desire to be loved.

The critics were there from the start. Many white South Africans simply loathed Tutu, seeing him as a popinjay who acted more like a rock star than a man of the cloth. But there were also critics within the antiapartheid movement. Some church members criticized Tutu for jumping around so much: taking one job, leaving it, and quickly starting another.

During the 1970s and 1980s, Tutu was the only major black South African spokesperson not in jail. This put a great burden on him, as he needed to be the voice for people like Nelson Mandela and Walter Sisulu, both of whom were held in prison on Robben Island (known in South African simply as "The Island"). Even his best friends sometimes felt he went too far in offering forgiveness to his foes and speaking of love and charity at a time when apartheid was being enforced more than ever. But Tutu received an enormous boost when Nelson Mandela, just freed from Robben Island, spent his first night of freedom at Tutu's Capetown residence.

we were, coming from all the different tribes and languages, diverse cultures and faith, so, utterly improbably, we were becoming one nation.[40]

In May 1994, Desmond Tutu administered the oath of office to Nelson Mandela as president of the new South Africa. This was a stunning moment, something for which black South Africans had waited their whole lifetimes.

Tutu and his wife, Leah, also had waited a long time for this moment. They hoped Desmond could soon retire, and they could have a peaceable and lasting retirement. As so often had been the case in the past, however, God had other plans.

During the early 1990s, Tutu himself acted more like the critic. He severely chastised the new administration of Nelson Mandela, claiming that all its members had gotten on board the gravy train before it left the station. Mandela and Tutu had moments of sharp disagreement, but they always reconciled; both men were very conscious of their need to act as a unified front.

Tutu came under the most severe criticism of his entire career during the meetings of the Truth and Reconciliation Commission. From the beginning, he acted in merciful and compassionate ways toward old leaders of the apartheid system—most notably to former President Botha. Many South Africans, white as well as black, thought Tutu was far too easy on his old foes, but if this was the greatest criticism that could be leveled against him, it surely stood well in comparison to what might have been.

Tutu never took criticism lightly. It pained him to receive it, but he manfully acted on what was pointed out to him. Whether as a parish priest, or as the leader of South Africa's Anglican community, he took plenty of heat. To his credit, he usually turned it around in a positive manner.

TRUTH AND RECONCILIATION COMMISSION

In 1995, President Nelson Mandela formally asked Desmond Tutu to become a leading member of the newly created Truth and Reconciliation Commission. Tutu may very well have wished to decline, but it was hard to refuse President Mandela in any matter, for Tutu had come to greatly admire and respect this man whose example in prison had set such a standard for the new nation. Tutu soon accepted his new role, and with 16 other members, he began to form the new commission.

Theirs was one of the hardest jobs that one can imagine. Each member of the commission knew, some from personal experience and some from reports, of the terrible things that happened during the many years of apartheid. Each member of the commission also knew that black South Africans wanted some form of revenge, some type of vengeance, against the leaders of the Afrikaner government who had allowed these things to happen. Yet that was not their task.

The job of the new commission was to find a balance between seeking the truth and letting the past go. As anyone who has ever had to forgive someone for a transgression knows, this is an exceedingly difficult task. As Desmond Tutu later said, it was not a matter of letting bygones be bygones. If someone has not apologized for what he or she has done, then it is not a matter of the past. It lives in the present.

CHAPTER 8

Hearing the Worst

Desmond Tutu was made chairperson of the new Truth and Reconciliation Commission (TRC). That he was the natural choice did not make the task any easier. His vice chairperson was a Methodist minister, Dr. Alex Boraine. Tutu and President Mandela made sure the commission was composed of people from all the different groups in South Africa.

The group began by setting some parameters. The TRC was authorized to look into all aspects of apartheid and the resistance to apartheid, but where should they begin? There were people still alive who were old enough to remember South Africa before apartheid began in 1948. Could their experiences also be used? Could they testify against the perpetrators of crimes committed so far back?

They decided to limit the scope of the commission to crimes committed between 1960, the year of the Sharpeville massacre, and 1994, when the first general free election took place. That was plenty of scope. Had the investigation gone back even farther, the commission might never have finished its work.

The commission had the power to subpoena witnesses, that is, to demand they appear, but it did not have the power to punish. It could make recommendations based on the testimony it heard. Many perpetrators could expect amnesty if they came forward and confessed to what they had done.

This was an essential element of the Truth and Reconciliation Commission. It was feared that if the commission was set up to judge and punish offenders, as the victorious Allies had done at the Nuremberg trials at the end of World War II. South Africa could have faced years of recriminations, and perhaps counterterrorism. Moreover, as Desmond Tutu pointed out, black South Africans had not won the struggle against apartheid in a military sense. The two sides had been deadlocked, and then apartheid had fallen of its own weight.

The commission began hearing testimony early in 1996. Even knowledgeable people, such as Desmond Tutu, and others who thought themselves hardened, were shocked by the extent to which violence had dominated South African life for the past three generations.

One man, who had been a security guard on Robben Island, confessed to having added bits of poison to the food eaten by Nelson Mandela. Fortunately, the activity had been botched, and Mandela's health had not been ruined. This was one of the lesser crimes heard of by Tutu and his fellow commissioners, however.

THE HORRORS OF APARTHEID

Tutu knew about many crimes committed before the commission began, but even he would be shocked by the list and litany of what came out during the hearings: "All South Africans know that our recent history is littered with some horrendous occurrences—the Sharpeville and Langdon killings, the Soweto uprising, the Church Street bombing, Mother Goose bar."[41] Tutu went on to describe the philosophy under which the commission operated:

> The past, it has been said, is another country. The way its sto-
> ries are told and the way they are heard change as the years go
> by. The spotlight gyrates, exposing old lies and illuminating
> new truth. As a fuller picture emerges, a new piece of the jigsaw
> puzzle of our past settles into place.[42]

The atrocities were so many and sometimes so horrible that they were difficult to believe. South African police and military personnel came forward to testify that they had tortured people, murdered them, doused their bodies with gasoline, and then set them afire. One thing Tutu had *not* known was that a human body takes about six hours to burn fully, and that many of the perpetrators had stood by, calmly watching the entire process. They wanted no record left of their hideous deeds.

On one occasion, in one of the early sessions, Tutu broke down and sobbed in response to what he heard. He became angry with himself, and with the press for making a big deal of this. He resolved never to weep again during the proceedings, no matter how horrific the testimony.

At first, many white South Africans were reluctant to come forward. They suspected the hearings were a sham and the amnesty promised would not be forthcoming. But, over the next year, a number of police and security personnel began to testify. As long as they told the whole truth, they were to receive amnesty. There was to be no retribution for what they had done between 1960 and 1994, so long as everything was brought to the light of day. Some of the most horrendous crimes had been perpetrated upon young people, even children.

The black pride or black resistance movement had lost many of its mature leaders when Nelson Mandela and others were imprisoned on Robben Island in 1964. In the decade or so that followed, many of the new leaders were young—teenagers, in fact. Some of them told of horrific things such as torture and being kept in solitary confinement, which many believed was the worst punishment of all. This belief tended to confirm

Desmond Tutu's Ubuntu (brotherhood) philosophy that a "person is a person through other persons." No one can flourish on his or her own.

Testimony was given both by those who had suffered and those who had inflicted the pain. The commission had the power to demand that witnesses appear, but Tutu and his colleagues worked to ensure people would want to come and give testimony. One of the most stunning stories was told by a woman named Zahrah Narkedien. Arrested in 1986, she related:

> They wanted me to say certain things, so they tortured me for seven days and the only thing that really made me break in the end was when they threatened to go back to the house where my sister was staying with me and kidnap my four-year-old nephew Christopher, bring him to the thirteenth floor and drop him out of the window.[43]

Things only got worse:

> They started to realize that I was enduring that kind of abuse [because she could pray while they tortured her] so they started to take a plastic bag . . . then one person held both my hands down and the other put it on my head. Then they sealed it so that I wouldn't be able to breathe and kept it on for at least two minutes, by which time the plastic was clinging to my eyelids, my nostrils, my mouth and my whole body was going into spasms because I really couldn't breathe.[44]

Zahrah Narkedien survived seven months in jail, but she emerged a battered person:

> I'm out of prison now for more than seven . . . years, but I haven't recovered and I will never recover, I know I won't. . . . The first two years after my release I tried to be normal again and the more I struggle to be normal, the more disturbed I

[became]. I had to accept that I was damaged, part of my soul was eaten away by maggots, horrible as it sounds, and I will never get it back again.[45]

The American journalist Bill Moyers produced a documentary of the testimony for the Corporation for Public Broadcasting (*Facing the Truth*, which aired in March 1999). One woman he

Sarafina!

Some of the aspects of Zahrah Narkedien's story are reminiscent of the film *Sarafina!*, released in 1992.

The heroines are a middle-aged schoolteacher (played by Whoopi Goldberg) and a 16-year-old girl named Sarafina, played by Leleti Khumalo. The film is set in Soweto, around the time of the 1976 riots, but many of its elements pertain to the freedom struggle in other parts of South Africa.

The schoolteacher teaches her children aspects of African history they have never heard before; and the school authorities become alarmed. Police and military are introduced into the area when schoolchildren sing and dance their freedom songs, some of which they learned from the teacher.

Not surprisingly, the schoolteacher is taken away and quietly disappears. Sarafina is also detained after she witnesses the horrific burning of a police informant. This man had been notorious in the township for years; the children run him down, douse him with gasoline, and set him on fire (vivid testimony that horrible acts were committed on both sides of the struggle).

Sarafina manages to hold out against the interrogators until she learns they have killed her beloved schoolteacher. When asked why she clings to this teacher and her message, Sarafina simply says, "I loved her." Battered and bewildered, Sarafina emerges from jail. She returns to her township, and in one of the last scenes of the film, she and her (formerly optimistic) friends sing their defiant and joyous song "Freedom . . . is coming tomorrow!"

interviewed, Thandi, claimed she had been able to withstand torture and rape by removing her spirit from her body and watching what happened from the (relative) safety of a corner of the cell. This phenomenon is known to those who study the effects of post-traumatic stress disorder. She told Bill Moyers that she had yet to return to the cell to find and fetch her soul, that "it was still sitting in the corner where she left it."[46]

HORRORS OF THE RESISTANCE

Tutu and other commission members had decided there would be no whitewashing of the deeds of black South Africans. Everyone needed to know about the horrors committed by the agents of apartheid, and everyone had to know what agents of the black resistance had done, as well.

Some of these revelations were sad in the extreme. A few blacks had been captured by security forces and promised freedom if they would participate in apartheid crimes. Other blacks, however, had carried out bombings where many innocent people had been killed or wounded. Still others had engaged in black-on-black violence between 1990 and 1994.

One of the saddest, most mortifying cases was that of Nelson Mandela's wife, Winnie. Tutu had known Winnie for over 20 years. They lived on the same street in Soweto, and one of her children was his godchild. Tutu admired Winnie for all the courageous things she had done to resist apartheid, but even he had to admit she had gone too far.

Sometime in the late 1980s, a few years before her husband Nelson was released, Winnie Mandela gathered a group of Soweto youths about her home; they called themselves the Mandela United Football Team. The name was a sham. These young men went about the Soweto neighborhoods rounding up suspected police informers, beating them up, and sometimes killing them. One of the very worst cases involved a 14-year-old boy, "Stompie" Seipei, whom, it appears, Winnie Mandela calmly watched being killed.

These revelations had come out slowly in the time since the elections of 1994. Winnie and Nelson Mandela had separated in 1991 and were divorced in 1996. Some people now looked on her with great suspicion, but to others she remained the courageous "Mother of the Nation" who had held things together during the years that her husband was in jail. Desmond Tutu tended toward the latter belief. He believed in Winnie Mandela's innate goodness, just as he held this out for everyone else that he encountered. Tutu made a very direct appeal to Winnie:

> There are people out there who want to embrace you. I still embrace you because I love you and I love you very deeply. . . . I beg you, I beg you, please. I have not made any particular finding from what has happened here. I speak as someone who has lived in this community. You are a great person and you don't know how your greatness would be enhanced if you were to say sorry, things went wrong, forgive me. I beg you.[47]

Winnie Mandela's seven-day hearing was an exercise in frustration. Time and again Desmond Tutu implored Winnie to confess all that she had done and to show remorse. For the most part, she was defiant, refusing to answer some questions and claiming that the commission had no right to demand answers from her. Many people felt that Desmond Tutu let her off too easily, but the record shows he tried time and again to obtain her full confession—yet he failed. Winnie Mandela's testimony was perhaps the most controversial part of the commission's experience.

Dr. Alex Boraine, the vice chairman of the commission, was generally very supportive of Tutu, admiring his ability to win over even the hardest hearts. Dr. Boraine saw the confrontation with Winnie as an important failure, however:

Desmond Tutu is shown here shaking hands with Winnie Mandela on the second day of the TRC hearings. Tutu, who presided over the hearings, was devastated by the information that he was to hear about Mandela's activities during the struggle.

I was stunned as we left the stage, exhausted and troubled. I had no idea that Tutu was going to conclude the way he did, and I was still trying to come to terms with that. . . . His intimate relationship with the Mandela family in this instance was a disadvantage, and I think he should have been more circumspect and more judicial. His hugging of Madikizela-Mandela [Winnie's maiden name was Madikizela] during the hearing, and his declaration of love and admiration, left the Commission wide open to the charge of bias.[48]

The formal Truth and Reconciliation Commission's report commented on her seven-day hearing:

There can be no doubt that Ms. Madikizela-Mandela was central to the establishment and formation of the MUFC [Mandela

United Football Club]. Club members were involved in at least eighteen killings, for which many of them are still serving prison sentences Many of the operations which led to the killings were launched from her home. Witnesses who appeared before the Commission implicated her in having known of these matters, in having actively participated in assaults or in having assisted in cover-ups and obstructing the course of justice. She denied all these allegations.[49]

ORDERS FROM THE TOP

In the early part of the commission's hearings, the focus was on people who had done the dirty work on the ground. As time progressed, evidence began to come to light that some of the terrible crimes had been committed with full authorization from above. Desmond Tutu had no special ax to grind against either P.W. Botha or F.W. de Klerk, but the evidence clearly pointed to both men. There were bombings that police testified had been authorized by the two men.

F.W. de Klerk and Nelson Mandela had shared the Nobel Peace Prize in 1993. De Klerk was seen as a hero by many people around the world, though not quite as esteemed as Mandela. As for P.W. Botha, he was now an old and rather sick man. The commission might look bad if it seemed to be going after this man in his retired years.

Tutu was well aware of the conflicts and the possible implications. He managed to bring F.W. de Klerk to the commission, but the testimony was quite unsatisfactory. Tutu went to P.W. Botha's home several times, trying to get him to attend the commission hearings, but these attempts failed. The former prime minister and president agreed to answer questions in writing, and his long, self-justifying answers contributed little to the TRC. By then, Tutu might have wondered if he ought to have reconsidered agreeing to participate in the commission in the first place, but at least the process was coming to an end.

Just hours before the Truth and Reconciliation Commission's report was to be released, the African National Congress asked that many sections of the report—those that dealt with atrocities committed by the black resistance movement—be stricken from the document. This was a painful moment for Tutu and all the members of the commission. Dr. Boraine thought later:

> I was astonished that several of my colleagues supported the proposal and were apparently oblivious to the consequences. What was ultimately at stake was party loyalty on the one hand and even-handedness on the other. . . . My heart was in my mouth when the vote was deadlocked at seven for and seven against. Tutu, however, used his casting vote and the motion was defeated.[50]

How could they hold their heads high if they presented a report that was a whitewash? The commission held a long discussion and tense debate, followed by a vote. The members were deadlocked, with seven in favor of suppressing the evidence and seven against. Tutu cast the deciding vote: What had been found out concerning the African National Congress would appear in the final version.

On October 29, 1998, Desmond Tutu presented the five-volume report of the commission to President Nelson Mandela. Of the original 18 commissioners, 16 had served all the way through, even though they had experienced frustrations much like Desmond Tutu. Characteristically, Tutu tried to put a good face on the end results:

> We have been given a great privilege. It has been a costly privilege but one that we would not want to exchange for anything in the world. Some of us have already experienced something of a post-traumatic stress and have become more and more aware of just how deeply wounded we have all been; how wounded and broken we all are. Apartheid has affected us at a very deep level, more than we ever suspected. We in the commission

President Nelson Mandela accepts the TRC's final report from Tutu on October 29, 1998, above. The final report was presented unvarnished, despite appeals from the African National Congress that certain sections be deleted from the document.

have been a microcosm of our society, reflecting its alienation, suspicions and lack of trust in one another. Our earlier commission meetings were very difficult and filled with tension. God has been good and helping us to grow closer together. Perhaps we are a sign of hope that, if people from often hostile backgrounds could grow closer together, as we have done, then there is hope for South Africa, that we can become united. We have been called to be wounded healers.[51]

The work was done. The process of healing continued.

CHAPTER 9

Peace in Old Age

Desmond Tutu had been feeling his years for some time. He came from a society in which few people made it to old age, in which many succumbed to disease or violence long before their time. Even when he was chosen to be the head of the Truth and Reconciliation Commission, Tutu had commented that he felt he was getting old and it was time for the sidelines. Now he might finally have that opportunity.

Tutu's old age was full of consolations. His children thrived; so did his grandchildren. His beloved daughter had become a full priest in the Anglican Church. He and Leah appeared to be closer than ever as they celebrated their fiftieth wedding anniversary in 2005. At some point in the proceedings, as someone said "for better or worse," Leah said no, "for better and better."[52]

There were losses, though—the inevitable ones that accompany aging. Father Trevor Huddleston died in 1998. He had been Tutu's original mentor, and much of Tutu's life's work had been cast in Huddleston's mold. Sadly, Huddleston's last years were spent in a mixture of pain and near insanity because of the ravages of diabetes.

Desmond and Leah Tutu celebrate their golden wedding anniversary on July 2, 2005, at a service at the Holy Cross Anglican Church in Soweto, above. During the celebration, Leah corrected the statement "for better or worse" by replying, "for better and better."

In 1998, Tutu was diagnosed with prostate cancer, just as he was finishing the commission report. He responded to it in a fashion that seemed typical to those who truly knew him. He saw it as another one of the messages of God, more evidence that God is in charge and humans simply adjust and do the best they can. Tutu spoke to the media about the matter, encouraging other South African men to be tested frequently for prostate cancer and other illnesses:

> Yes, it would be nice to stick around a little longer. But I believe, as a Christian, that death is the end of one part, but the beginning of another. It's like a doorway passing from one room of God's wonderful world to another, where all the things that

drag you down won't be around. I would love to see my grand-children grow, but I've been richly blessed with wonderful friends all over the world.[53]

Desmond and Leah continued to travel during their old age. World travelers, they were now welcomed as heroes nearly every-where they went. They spent some time at Emory University in the southern part of the United States, and received honors from colleges and universities around the world. Even so, Tutu expe-rienced frustrations and had serious concerns about the state of world affairs. He knew he and his friends and partners had fought the great evil they had known—apartheid—but other evils seemed to loom on the horizon. All of Africa, but in particular, the southern, sub-Saharan region, has been seriously affected by AIDS (acquired immunodeficiency syndrome). Although this deadly disease has also spread in more developed areas, such as the United States and Western Europe, education, changes in lifestyle, and the development of effective medicines has blunted its impact there. By contrast, South Africa had many people practicing "unsafe" sex, and there were other factors present that contributed to the spread of AIDS. The disease now threatens to overwhelm whole sections of the country.

Tutu was also concerned about the growth of militarism, espe-cially that shown by the United States toward Saddam Hussein's Iraq. Tutu had always had ambivalent feelings about America: He loved its people and admired many of its institutions, but the administrations of Ronald Reagan and George H. W. Bush were not helpful toward black South Africans in their past struggles. Then, in 2003, President George W. Bush carried out an invasion of Iraq to topple the dictator Saddam Hussein.

Many people in America and Western Europe protested against that military action. On a cold day in February 2003, Tutu joined thousands of others outside the United Nations building in New York, chanting "Peace, Peace!" The American military invasion began the next month and quickly toppled Saddam

Hussein's government, but many Americans have since regretted the action, as establishing law and order in that country has proven difficult.

The Peacemaker's Successor

Everyone knew that Desmond Tutu would be a tough act to follow. The person who was chosen to succeed him as archbishop of Cape Town, put it this way in 1996:

> In my early days as Archbishop when the phone rang and people asked to speak to the Archbishop of Cape Town, I would set off to find him.*

Njongonkulu Ndungane came from circumstances rather like those of Desmond Tutu. His father was a black priest in a very poor parish. Ndungane did not expect to seek holy orders himself; as a young man he became a radical in favor of social change in South Africa (the same could be said of many others who later became responsible leaders). Because of his outspokenness, Ndungane went to the infamous prison on Robben Island between 1963 and 1966; he was one of the workers who built the prison that later incarcerated Nelson Mandela.

Ndungane experienced the worst that Robben Island had to offer, and, instead of breaking him, it convinced him of the necessity of a God-driven path. He studied for the Anglican priesthood soon after his release, and, like Desmond Tutu, he spent some time abroad, primarily in Great Britain. By the time he met Tutu in the late 1970s, Ndungane was on a similar wavelength with his more famous colleague. The two worked together many times over the years, and, in 1996, Ndungane became the new archbishop of Cape Town.

To those who listen to his speeches, or read his book *A World with a Human Face*, Ndungane comes across as more "hard-headed" and practical than Desmond Tutu. There is the same emphasis on God's love, and on the need for human charity, but Ndungane also ventures much farther into economics and social conditions than Tutu had. One might say that each

As he approached his seventy-fifth birthday, Tutu showed no signs of slowing down. He served a number of one-semester appointments at American universities, then crossed the ocean

great leader, such as a churchman, has to confront what he sees as the greatest evil of his time, and to Ndungane, poverty is that enemy.

He has called on European and American governments to forgive debts from African countries as a whole and South Africa in particular. Only through having a clean slate will Africa be able to rise to her potential, he says. Ndungane has been very critical of international organizations like the World Bank, claiming they receive far more from Third World nations than they give. Ndungane has been critical of globalization from the start, saying that its values, ideas, and beliefs are essentially the product of one group of people—upper class people in modern, Westernized nations—and that the whole spectrum of humanity has yet to be heard from (in this he sounds like Desmond Tutu, who spoke many times of the "rainbow peoples of God").

Issues of homosexuality and AIDS have played a major part in Nbungane's tenure as archbishop. When he became archbishop, the number of cases of AIDS and HIV were high and on the rise, but they have since escalated exponentially. Ndungane has been a champion of social and sexual reform, insisting that his flock pay greater attention both to the importance of sexuality and to the need to behave responsibly with the power it brings.

Like Tutu, Njongonkulu Ndungane has a rich and sometimes bewildering heritage on which to draw. He is an African, a South African, a black person, and an Anglican leader, all rolled into one. Like Tutu, he believes in the old African concept of Ubuntu, meaning that a person is a person because of his or her relationship with other persons.

---

*Njongonkulu Ndungane, *A World With a Human Face: A Voice from Africa.* World Council of Churches, 2003, p. 18.

to teach at King's College in London, where his academic career flourished so many years ago.

Tutu now had time to put together his comprehensive philosophy. That it was a very personal philosophy surprised no one. In several books written at the beginning of the twenty-first century, Tutu reiterated his belief that God knows people one by one and name by name. Tutu believed in a deeply personal God who looks upon humans as his finest experiment. There were plenty of reasons why God might despair over the state of humanity, but Tutu saw hope in any situation:

> What we are, what we have, even our salvation, all this gift, all his grace, is not to be achieved but to be received as a gift freely given. God's bias in favor of sinners is so immense that it is said we will be surprised that those who find in heaven whom we had not expected to encounter there. Ultimately, no one is an irredeemable cause, devoid of all hope.[54]

Not everyone would agree. Although Desmond Tutu liked to speak of the many times during the commission hearings in which victims chose to forgive perpetrators, there were probably just as many times when someone could not or would not forgive.

Desmond Tutu has had many critics over the years. Very few ever accused him of corruption or of bad intentions, but many believe he let the perpetrators of the crimes of apartheid escape too lightly. Tutu took these criticisms seriously, but he never wavered from his basic philosophy, which was that there was good in each and every person, and that all played a role in God's plan. Tutu is an extraordinary leader of his time. Together with a handful of other religious leaders, he played a role in bringing down major forces of oppression.

THREE TITANS OF FAITH

At the turn of the twenty-first century, Desmond Tutu, the Dalai Lama, and Pope John Paul II were the three most recognizable

The Dalai Lama (right) shares a light moment with Desmond Tutu during talks with journalists in Cape Town on August 21, 1996. The two men share a devotion to their respective religions, which has aided each of them in their struggles against oppression.

religious figures in the world. Pope John Paul II was instrumental in bringing the curtain down on Soviet Communism; likewise, His Holiness the Dalai Lama (whose core message is quite similar to Tutu's) has illuminated the plight of the Tibetan people. Desmond Tutu deserves to stand among these other giants of faith and reconciliation toward the end of the twentieth century.

Desmond Tutu had his first meeting with Pope John Paul II in 1983. Each knew what it was like to struggle against an oppressive government. John Paul had gone underground to escape the Nazis in World War II. Like John Paul, Tutu battled for many years against an oppressive regime. John Paul had greater resources to draw on—those of the Vatican—and he was not oppressed within the borders of his own country. As difficult a life as Tutu sometimes had within the borders of South Africa, though, the Dalai Lama has had a still harder road, having spent two-thirds of his life in political exile.

It is unknown when Tutu first met the Dalai Lama, but the two have been great friends ever since. Each delights in playing practical jokes, and both like to tell stories that seem to reflect poorly on themselves. Tutu's Ubuntu philosophy of brotherhood is rather similar to that of the Dalai Lama. Both men believe that we are nothing outside of relationship, though the Dalai Lama might well say that relationships can be with many things, whereas Desmond Tutu would argue strongly in favor of *human* connection.

One thing is certain. All three of these men fought battles against oppression, and all kept their integrity and spirit alive, even in the most difficult of times.

1902	Anglo-Boer War ends with British victory.
1910	Union of South Africa is formed.
1912	African National Congress is formed.
1931	Desmond Tutu is born in Klerksdorp, South Africa.
1942	Tutu family moves to Krugersdorp.
1943	Father Trevor Huddleston arrives in South Africa.
1945	World War II ends in Europe and the Pacific.
1946	Desmond Tutu comes down with tuberculosis.
1948	He makes a full recovery.
1948	The National Party wins the general elections; apartheid begins.
1949	Tutu enters the Bantu Normal School in Pretoria.
1952	Major black protests against apartheid are held.
1955	Tutu marries Leah Shenxane and begins teaching.
1956	Father Huddleston leaves South Africa; he publishes *Naught for Your Comfort*.
1958	Tutu enters theological training.
1960	Peaceful black demonstrators are massacred at Sharpeville; African National Congress is banned by South African government.
1961	Tutu and family go to England.
1962	Albert Luthuli's *Let My People Go* is published.
1963	Albert Luthuli wins the Nobel Peace Prize but cannot attend the ceremony.

1964	Nelson Mandela and other ANC leaders are sentenced to life in prison.
1966	Tutu and family return to South Africa; Tutu teaches at Alice.
1970	Tutu becomes lecturer at University of Botswana.
1972	He becomes director of the World Theological Fund.
1975	He becomes dean of Johannesburg.
1976	The Soweto riots take place; Tutu is enthroned as bishop of Lesotho.
1977	Steven Biko is murdered.
1978	Tutu becomes general secretary of the South African Council of Churches.
1980	Tutu meets Prime Minister P.W. Botha for first time.
1981	Ronald Reagan becomes president of the United States.
1984	State of emergency is called in South Africa; Tutu wins the Nobel Peace Prize.
1985	Tutu becomes bishop of Johannesburg.
1986	Tutu becomes bishop of Cape Town.
1988	Film *Cry Freedom* is released.
1989	Trevor Huddleston leads the "Freedom at 70" movement. Eastern European countries overthrow Communist governments.
1990	Nelson Mandela is released from prison.
1991	Tutu sounds alarm about increasing violence.

1992 Split occurs between Zulu leader Buthelezi and African National Congress; Film *Sarafina!* is released.

1993 It is agreed that elections will take place.

1994 Elections are held in April; Nelson Mandela becomes first president of a new South Africa.

1995 Tutu and 16 others are named to the Truth and Reconciliation Commission (TRC).

1996 TRC hearings begin.

1997 Tutu is diagnosed with prostate cancer.

1998 TRC releases its final report.

1999 Tutu's *No Future Without Forgiveness* is published; Trevor Huddleston dies in Britain.

2004 Tutu's *God Has a Plan* is published.

2005 Desmond and Leah celebrate their fiftieth wedding anniversary.

NOTES

Chapter 1

1. Desmond Tutu, *The Rainbow People of God: The Making of a Peaceful Revolution*. John Allen, ed. New York: Doubleday, 1994, pp. 6–7.
2. Ibid., p. 7.
3. Ibid., p. 9.
4. Ibid., p. 10.
5. Ibid., p. 11.
6. Ibid., p. 12.
7. Ibid.

Chapter 2

8. Trevor Huddleston, *Naught for Your Comfort*. New York: Doubleday, 1956, p. 121.
9. Ibid.
10. Ibid., p. 131.
11. Shirley Du Boulay, *Tutu: Voice of the Voiceless*. Grand Rapids, MI: Eerdmans Publishing, 1988, p. 31.

Chapter 3

12. Ibid., p. 43.
13. Huddleston, *Naught for Your Comfort*, p. 190.
14. Du Boulay, *Tutu: Voice of the Voiceless*, pp. 58–59.
15. Ibid., p. 62.

Chapter 4

16. Desmond Tutu, *God Has A Dream: A Vision of Hope for Our Time*. New York: Doubleday, 2004, p. 25.
17. Ibid., p. 32.

18. Tutu, *The Rainbow People of God*, p. 16.
19. Ibid.
20. Ibid., p. 20.
21. Ibid., p. 21.

Chapter 5

22. Du Boulay, *Tutu: Voice of the Voiceless*, p. 121.
23. Ibid., p. 141.
24. Ibid.
25. Tutu, *The Rainbow People of God*, p. 86.
26. Ibid., p. 87.
27. Ibid., p. 89.
28. Ibid., pp. 90–91.
29. Ibid., p. 94.
30. Ibid., p. 94.

Chapter 6

31. Alan Cowell, "Tutu Installed as Bishop; Defends Political Role," *New York Times*, February 4, 1985, p. 3.
32. Alan Cowell, "Bishop Tutu Saves Man From Crowd," *New York Times*, July 11, 1985, p. 3.
33. Ibid.
34. Ibid.
35. Tutu, *God Has A Dream*, pp. 43–44.
36. Artists Against Apartheid, *Sun City*.

Chapter 7

37. Tutu, *The Rainbow People of God*, p. 228.
38. Ibid., p. 229.

39. Ibid., p. 231.
40. Tutu, *God Has a Dream*, p. 7.

Chapter 8

41. *Truth and Reconciliation Commission of South Africa Report*, Vol. 1. Cape Town, South Africa, 1998, p. 1.
42. Ibid., p. 4.
43. Desmond Tutu, *No Future Without Forgiveness*. New York: Doubleday, 1999, p. 138.
44. Ibid., p. 139.
45. Ibid., pp. 140–141.
46. Ibid., p. 141.
47. Steven D. Gish, *Desmond Tutu: A Biography*. Greenwood Press, 2004, p. 155.
48. Alex Boraine, *A Country Unmasked*. Oxford University Press, 2000, pp. 252–253.

49. *Truth and Reconciliation Commission of South Africa Report*, Vol. 1, p. 22; Vol 2., p. 581.
50. Boraine, *A Country Unmasked*, p. 307.
51. *Truth and Reconciliation Commission of South Africa Report*, Vol. 1., p. 22.

Chapter 9

52. "Tutu and Wife Celebrate 50th Anniversary." Available at http://www.boston.com/news/world/africa/articles/2005/07/03/tutu_wife_celebrate_50th_anniversary/.
53. "There's Life After Prostate Cancer," *Ebony*, 1998.
54. Tutu, *God Has A Dream*, p. 85.

BIBLIOGRAPHY

Books

Boraine, Alex. *A Country Unmasked*. New York: Oxford University Press, 2000.

Denniston, Robin. *Trevor Huddleston: A Life*. New York: St. Martins Press, 1999.

Du Boulay, Shirley. *Tutu: Voice of the Voiceless*. Grand Rapids, MI: Eerdmans Publishing,1988.

Gish, Steven D. *Desmond Tutu: A Biography*. Westport, CT: Greenwood Press, 2004.

Huddleston, Trevor. *Naught for Your Comfort*. New York: Doubleday, 1956.

Luthuli, Albert. *Let My People Go*. New York: McGraw-Hill, 1962.

Temkin, Ben. *Buthelezi: A Biography*. London: Frank Cass, 2003.

Truth and Reconciliation Commission of South Africa Report (5 vols). Cape Town, South Africa, 1998.

Tutu, Desmond. *God Has a Dream: A Vision of Hope for Our Time*. New York: Doubleday, 2004.

———. *No Future Without Forgiveness*. New York: Doubleday, 1999.

———. *The Rainbow People of God: The Making of a Peaceful Revolution*, John Allen, ed. New York: Doubleday, 1994.

Newspapers and Magazines

Cheers, D. Michael. "There's Life After Prostate Cancer." *Ebony*, February 1998, p. 70.

Cowell, Alan. "Bishop Tutu Saves Man From Crowd." *New York Times,* July 11, 1985.

Cowell, Alan. "Tutu Installed as Bishop, Defends Political Role." *New York Times*, February 4, 1985.

Daley, Suzanne. "South Africa Truth Commission May Withhold Its Report." *New York Times*, October 29, 1998.

Greenwald, John. "Searching for New Worlds." *Time*, October 28, 1984.

Russell, George. "Railing Against Racism." *Time*, December 24, 1984.

FURTHER READING

Du Boulay, Shirley. *Tutu: Voice of the Voiceless*. Grand Rapids, MI: Eerdmans Publishing, 1988.

Gish, Steven D. *Desmond Tutu: A Biography*. Westport, CT: Greenwood Press, 2004.

Huddleston, Trevor. *Naught for Your Comfort*. New York: Doubleday, 1956.

Reader's Digest. *Illustrated History of South Africa: The Real Story*. Pleasantville, NY: Reader's Digest Press, 1988.

Web sites

Testimony of Narkedien and Others at the Truth and Reconciliation Commission Hearings.
http://www.sabctruth.co.za/slicesright.htm

"The Life and Work of Archbishop Trevor Huddleston." African National Congress.
http://www.anc.org.za/ancdocs/history/solidarity/huddlebio.html.

"Tutu and Wife Celebrate 50th Anniversary." Boston.com.
http://www.boston.com/news/world/africa/articles/2005/07/03/tutu_wife_celebrate_50th_anniversary/

PICTURE CREDITS

page

2 AFP/Getty Images
5 AFP/Getty Images
11 Getty Images
19 AFP/Getty Images
26 Time & Life Pictures/Getty
Images
28 Getty Images
41 Getty Images
46 Getty Images
60 AFP/Getty Images

63 Associated Press, AP
67 Associated Press, AP
69 Associated Press, AP
73 Associated Press, AP
75 Associated Press, AP
86 Associated Press, AP
89 Associated Press, AP
92 Associated Press, AP
97 Associated Press, AP

cover Associated Press, AP

INDEX

SAMUEL WILLARD CROMPTON lives in the Berkshire Hills of western Massachusetts. He is a historian and biographer with a special interest in spirituality, especially as it relates to modern-day struggles. His extensive writing for Chelsea House includes biographies of Emanuel Swedenborg, Jonathan Edwards, and Saint Thomas More.